Talking to the Dead, Fortune and Future Telling

From the past to the present
A look at the history of how it started and what is still working

Shirley Scott

Animal Communicator/Psychic

I asked for the help of others to write this book because I don't use many of these tools for my readings. I rely on my spirit guides and the messages I get from helpers on the other side.

 I wanted to get information out about how other people work with some of the tools and/or practices in this book. I wanted to find out how they may use these tools or practices to help guide themselves or others on their life paths. As with any tool, nothing is always 100% correct. Even the best psychic is never correct all the time.   This is because everything can change with our choices and we all have free will.. And sometimes we just have to walk through a lesson to learn from it without knowing what is coming.

Some of these tools and practices are very old and are either not used today or used in a very limited way. I am NOT endorsing any of them. What I am doing is bringing out information about how these are used and what the users think they do for them.

When you are working with some of these tools, remember that there is nothing better than your own intuitive feelings or messages. These are just tools to help receive messages. However, your gut and heart are very important to listen to as you walk through your life. They are really your psychic connection to everything in this world and beyond.

When someone is using these tools, the message can be and usually is their interpretation. If it doesn't feel right to you, then don't listen to it. When I'm doing a psychic reading, I get out of my way and just let the messages come through. This is what a good reader does, no matter what tool they are using.

It's fun to use these tools and most of them have roots from hundreds or even thousands of years ago. The more these tools are used, the more you or the users are putting energy into the tool. This is good and bad. It can create problems unless the user cleans and clears the energy around these items after each use.

Most of these tools will tell you what MIGHT happen but nothing is written in stone. Let the messages be a guide for you, not an absolute path. These tools should be used as fence post markers to help you see what might be coming, how to handle it and seeing the positive in all of it.

If the user has nothing but negative things to say, run as fast as you can. No matter what is happening in your life, there is always a way to find something positive.

As you read through this book, remember to keep an open mind, positive thoughts and feel in your body how you are feeling about any of these tools.

Some people will want to explore or experiment with some of these tools and that's great. However, these are just tools and not always the answer. Also it can take years of practice to get comfortable with a tool or get it to work right for you.

This book is a book to inform. To make you think. To help you understand what tools, intention and energy can and cannot do for you. It is to help open your eyes to possibilities and pitfalls.

The stories and information from other people in this book are their experiences and their thoughts. You don't have to agree or disagree. You might only keep an open mind and if you want to learn more on one of the tools, then you should read and learn about it.

I call "all that is" the Mystery because we certainly don't understand all there is to know about energy, our soul, being connected and everything that is in this galaxy and Universe. Everything is connected, from the stars to Earth, rocks to plants, humans to humans to animals. None of us are alone or not connected to "all" that is in our galaxy and beyond.

(I take no credit or responsibility for the chapters and information in this book that I didn't personally write or research. The chapters written by other people are their views, experiences, opinions and the information they work with.)

Psychic Readings

No one knows just how long psychics have been around or how long they have been doing readings. My belief is that we are all psychic and intuitive in our own way. I believe that when humans came to Earth, we brought gifts with us to help us on this planet.

Psychics or seers seem to be mentioned as far back as recorded time. In ancient Egypt the high priests cherished the Book of the Dead. They believed that many high priests got their messages from the gods and shared them with the people.

In Greek mythology the goddess of the soul Psykhe, traveled back and forth between this world and the underworld get receive messages from the dead. This was considered being 'psychic'.

Nostradamus was a very famous astrologer and seer whose writings are still popular today. He was considered 'psychic'.

The 'evil eye', which is usually associated with the middle of the forehead and psychic awareness, was feared in many ancient counties. Even today we say that we need to open our third eye to help our psychic powers. This third eye is located in the middle of the forehead.

Psychic readers have been feared, loved and mostly judged by people that don't really understand the gift. Psychics are either loved or hated depending on the era and/or the country. So the history of being psychic or a seer as being a natural way to get information probably dates back to prehistoric man.

I'm wanted to start this book with psychic readings because this is what I do. I read humans and do animal communication with all kinds of animals. I don't use any of the tools that we are going to be looking at in this book, but that doesn't mean they don't help with information. I have used and studied many of the tools in this book but personally I do better with just my spirit guides. I find most of them very interesting and I understand how the unseen world of spirit can work through them to get messages to us.

I'm going to tell you how I work so you can see that everyone gets their messages differently and none of these ways of receiving messages are wrong. This will also show you that when someone tells you that you have to do something a certain way or it won't work, they are probably wrong.

I don't tell people that they have to meditate for hours to be connected to the Universe or be psychic. I don't meditated much but I'm still psychic. That is my purpose in this life. I never say, "Well if you don't get messages the same way I do, you're wrong." Everyone will get their messages in a different way.

Some people will be like me and see pictures, hear words, get a gut feeling, have pain in my body or even get smells. I'm honored to be able to get my messages in several different ways. However, there are many people who don't see pictures, they might just hear words. Or some people just a feeling and know that something will happen.

It is also important to understand your individual gift and to learn to work with it. There are some people that see bloody events that might happen or they see demons and monsters. There are controls to help people with this type of message receiving. You don't have to see blood or guts to get the message.

After my near death out-of-body experience, I went to a psychic school for a year to learn how to control and understand what I was hearing and seeing. It helped so much to understand my gift and learn how I could control it.

I would suggest to everyone who is struggling with a spiritual gift to contact a person who has been doing readings or helping people for a long time. I help people do this. It's not an overnight, immediate understanding but I do guide people so they have the tools to use when events or messages get overwhelming.

When I first started doing readings, the Universe pushed me into it full force. Before I was finished with my first year at school, I was doing readings for people. Here is a funny story that helped me help others.

While I was in psychic school, I meant a man. I didn't like this man and I knew he was bad news but something told me there was something there for me to learn. I didn't know when I meant him that he was in trouble with the law, smoked pot and was a drinker. He was everything I wasn't.

I really didn't like the guy at all. However we started dating as he was very persuasive and as I look back on it now, I bet he could sell ice cubes to a polar bear. We only dated two months but that was more than enough for me.

I was out of work at the time so everywhere we went he would introduce me as his psychic girlfriend. He would then ask the person if they wanted a reading and told them how much it would cost. Most of these people were strangers on the street. I was always so embarrassed and because I was new at giving readings I really lacked confidence. However, he was the one that got me out of my shell and into reading people.

So you may never know why you meet someone until after the fact and you have stepped back at looked at it with different eyes.

Another interesting story is how I became an animal communicator. After just a year or so of doing human readings, one of my friends said to me, "If you can do humans, you can do animals."

Well, I had never really thought about it. I had always loved animals and my mother never knew what I would bring home next when I was young. My friend's comment made me think and wonder if that was possible.

The next weekend I went with her to a dog show. She was a vendor there and said to me, "Just come and sit in my booth and quietly talk to the dogs and see what you get."

I figured there was no harm in doing that so we started walking around before the show started. She suggested we walk toward the groomer's tent and if a dog came toward us, I could just talk to them to see what I get and no one would be the wiser. That made sense to me. When a dog would come near us, I would send out a telepathic message to it. I was amazed at the pictures and messages they were sending back to me and before I knew it we were in front of the groomer's tent.

As we entered the groomer's tent, it was like entering a crowded room where everyone, humans and dogs were talking. I continued to send out messages to some of the dogs and was surprised I was getting many answers back from them. I was very connected to the dogs and was almost unaware of what the humans and my friend were doing.

I was in a deep conversation with a poodle when all of a sudden my friend shouted out, "Excuse me everyone. Today in my booth is a world known animal communicator. She will be doing readings in my booth all day today and tomorrow. So come on over and sign up. There is a charge so bring your cash or check book."

I was standing there with my mouth open staring at my friend. I'm sure I looked like a deer in the headlights. She whispered, "Smile – you have their attention."

I tried to smile and look normal but I was in a cold panic. Needless to say, the rest of the next two days were spent communicating with dogs and helping their owners understand them. This was the beginning of my animal communication.

After that day, I never looked back. Now, over twenty years later I read animals and humans from all over the world.

If I had to tell someone one thing to do to get better at receiving messages, it would be to listen to your inner guidance and practice every day. This is not something you can use once a year and expect it to be perfect. I have at between one to five readings every day of the year. I have learned to live in the present moment like animals do. I've learned to talk to my spirit guides and I do it every day. Speaking to my guides and getting better at understanding them helps me hear the messages when they are talking to me.

If you are going to use one of the tools in this book, practice is the most important part of learning. Learn how it works for you and only for you. Don't try to be anyone but you.

I've had people say, "I want to do what you do. How do I do that?" I tell them they do that by being themselves.

I don't do a regular meditation. When I feel like I need to sit down and be quiet, I do that. I do have my own agreements with my spirit guides that we made years ago. They talk through me when someone calls for a reading. I never remember my readings because it's not me that is giving a message. It is spirit guides and angels. Plus with as many readings as I give each week, month and year, I'd go crazy trying to remember them.

It's best not to remember any of them because it means my human self can't get in the way of the information that is coming through from the other side of the veil or the Universe. In other words, I don't think about what is being said so I can't put a judgment on any part of the reading.

When I'm giving a reading, I'm in touch with the client's energy and higher self and my spirit guide. When the client asks me a question, I usually hear something or get a picture from my spirit guide. These are the main two ways I get my answers.

When I'm asked a medical problem, I can usually feel the pain where the client is feeling it, whether it's a human or animal. I don't diagnose illnesses but feeling the pain can help my client get to the right health care provider. Also, knowing where your animal's pain is can help the vet look at that area first.

Animals know many things but they don't know what the word cancer means unless we train them. They will smell an illness and point it out but they don't know what that illness might be until we teach them. Then they will associate the smell with the word we use. They can smell fear, happiness, sadness and all our emotions too. Each emotion has its own vibration and smell.

When animals "talk" to me they let me know how
they are feeling and when they are in certain moods or
if they are not feeling well.

When you get a psychic reading, there are a few
things you need to think about.

First - Price doesn't equal quality. In fact, it has been
my experience, that many people who charge too
much aren't that good.

Second - the psychic should act like they have your
soul in their hands, because in many cases they do.
They need to make you feel like you are the most
important person in the world. They should let you
know that there are no dumb or unimportant
questions.

Third - If something doesn't feel right to you, then
don't take it in. If a psychic says something that you
"feel" is wrong, walk away. There are too many
psychics now that put their emotions or life
experiences on you. Like I stated earlier, I stand by
the wayside when I'm doing a reading and just let my
guides speak through me. I rarely remember what I
tell someone because it's not me telling them and I
don't let my emotions get in the way.

Fourth - Nothing is set in stone. If a psychic says
something is going to happen, you can change it by
either changing your mind or your actions. An

example is if you are told you are going to die in a
green truck on Monday, don't get into a green truck
on any Monday.

Fifth - When a message comes through from another
dimension, there can be a misunderstanding. The
vibrations from one dimension to another can distort
words or pictures.

Sixth - Sometimes a psychic will be seeing things far
into the future and not just in a few months or a year.
There is no time or space in some dimensions so a
psychic might see things that could take years to come
true. They may not realize that they are seeing ten
years out instead of two years.

Last but not least, a psychic should always have a
positive side to any reading. No reading should put
you in fear. Fear is a way many psychics get clients to
come back over and over again. The client comes
back in hopes the future will be better but the psychic
will continue to put fear in them so they will keep
coming back. So if a psychic tells you the future is
bleak, find someone else.

Psychic readings are a good way to check to see if
you are on your path. You can check in on your
future, your finances, your relationship, your health
and many other things you are worried about.
However always keep in mind that you are in control

of your life, not a psychic. You are the one that
should make all the choices and no one should try to
take away your free will.

We all have some kind of psychic or intuitive power.
Some of us are meant to help people with it and some
are just to use it for themselves. Whatever you decide
to do with your gift, be sure to use it for good and
positive outcomes.

Doing psychic readings is my calling in this life and I
take it very serious.

But no matter what you do with your gift, never use
it for evil or to hurt people. Karma's a bitch.

I hope that answers some questions about how to
use a psychic reading to help you on your path.
Always pick someone you are comfortable with and
who you feel has the best intention for you.

Using a Crystal Ball

The use of crystal balls for fortune telling dates back to the ancient and mysterious Druids and the practice of scrying.   This practice involved starring into a reflective surface, such as a pond or shiny stone. They thought if they looked into it long enough, visions would appear that would help them either tell the future or answer their questions. Later many other cultures adopted and used scrying for thousands of years.

The Druids would share their visions with other people in the area. These pictures helped to make important decisions and advise other people. It was the Druids that crafted the use of gemstones and made the first crystal balls. This race of people was known to be storytellers, advisers, healers and spiritual leaders to not only their own people but to others as well.

Druids walked the Earth as early as the 3rd century BCE. The word Druid is a Celtic term that means "Knowing the oak tree". This name for these people was probably born because they performed rituals in the oak forests that were near their village.

The Druids would go in the oak forests and stare into the ponds that were in the woods. They believed they would see glimpses of the future. They would then come back to the village and enlighten people as to what they saw. It was quite mysterious back in those days and people looked at the Druids as souls that were connected to the gods.

When the Romans over took the British Isles, where the Druids lived, they killed most of the Druid people out of fear of their mystical power. As the Romans destroyed this civilization, they also destroyed the Druid's mystical and spiritual practices.

In the book "The Natural History" Pling the Elder wrote a whole chapter on the Druids and their magic. This book was one of the first books to mention crystal balls and how they were used.

The practices and beliefs of the Druid people were in direct opposition with the teachings of Christianity. The practice of scrying with crystal balls was condemned by the church and it was a crime if you got caught doing it. The church claimed it was directly linked to the devil.

In the 5th century book, "The City of God", St. Augustine stated that using a crystal ball is a way to be "entangled in the deceptive rites of crystal balls versus Christianity."

Prcatrix, an Arabic writer during the Renaissance era, looked at mysticism as a true science. He advocated for it to be a branch of science. He wrote about scrying as a logical and scientific practice. His writings made many European scholars take another look at scrying. This new interest on the practice of scrying made it popular among the academic and elite classes. This was the beginning of bringing the practice of scrying back to life.

It was during this time, the 8th to the 10th centuries CE, that many Roma people came to Europe. The Roma people originated in the Punjab region of Northern India and were nomadic people with very different religion beliefs. Many were already practicing fortune telling before they migrated to Europe.

The Roma people instantly become at odds with the Catholic Church. The church ostracized the Roma people and this is where the name "gypsy" came to be.

The Roma people, or gypsies, were extreme believers in fortune telling. Because jobs were hard to come by and the Catholic Church made it even harder for them to work, the gypsies turned to fortune telling to make a living.

These were desperate times and the gypsies would charge for fortune telling. Fortune telling became a big business and income for the Roma people. Because the European people already knew about the crystal balls and the mysticism that surrounded them, the gypsies started using crystal balls as a tool to appear more mysterious.

Also, the crystal balls were small and portable. They were easy to pack and take with them. This way they could set up a fortune telling stand anywhere and everywhere they went. They had to keep moving because if they were in one spot too long, the church would have them arrested.

Today crystal balls aren't used very much. It seems that starring into a crystal ball has lost its mystery or maybe it's just that people aren't able to see anything in them. It could take from a few minutes to hours before a vision might appear in the ball. It's also believed that the user of a crystal ball probably had some kind of psychic ability too. Today crystal balls are viewed more as a pretty center piece that adds magic to a room instead of a tool to tell your fortune.

If you want to use a crystal ball, it will take practice to be able to see visions and then to interpret them into fortune telling. It might be fun to glaze into one to see what you get but until you have a few years under your belt, I would be careful about what your visions might mean.

Tea Leaf Readings
(Also coffee ground or wine sediment)

The reading of tea leaves is known as tasseography. It is said that tea leaf readings have their beginnings in Asia. While China was using tea leaves, Ancient Greece and the Middle Eastern culture were using coffee grounds and wine sediment. All of these elements are read basically the same way so we will stick with tea leafs as this is used the most throughout the world.

When tea from China was introduced to Europe, about the 17th century, the Europeans started using tea also.

For many years tea was a drink for only the rich. As tea spread throughout Europe, it became more affordable and almost everyone could enjoy a cup at tea time.

About this time more people were getting together to discuss everything from world developments to personal issues over a cup of tea. People began to see the tea leaves were reflecting their discussions and situations. It was much like seeing different shapes in clouds or in water and we feel these images are messages given to us from the other side.

The Romani people are credited with spreading tea leaf readings throughout Europe. They would go door to door to ask people if they would like their tea leaves read. By the end of the 1800's, the Romani people had set up tea parlors and tea rooms and were offering guests paid tea leaf readings. Many Romani people were reading the future and making a small fortune.

About that same time, tea was becoming popular in the US. People were openly using tea parlors by the mid 1800's. By WWI many American women had their own parlors. They would serve a light snack while serving tea. Then they would read the leaves which enhanced the experience and kept many coming back for more.

Tea leaf readings and the instructions on how to do them were passed down from mother to daughter for generations. Most people agree that to read tea leaves well the reader needs a level of clairvoyance.

The following is a typical tea leaf reading.

First of course you have to brew a cup of tea. You can't use tea bags. You need to use loose cut tea leaves. They should be dark in color and the cup needs to be light colored so the leaves can be easily read.

The person who is going to be read should drink the tea and be thinking of a question they want to ask. It's important to focus on the intention and put energy into the question. It should be one question and it should not be changed during the drinking of the tea or reading of the leaves. It is also important to have a clear and concise question. If the question is to general, the answer will also be general.

Drink the tea down and leave about a tablespoon of tea at the bottom of the cup. Then the "consultant" or "sitter" or "querent", which is the person receiving the reading, should take the cup by the handle in their left hand and move it in a circular motion three times from left to right to allow some of the tea leaves to cling to the side of the cup while others remain at the bottom.

Then invert the cup over a saucer so the remaining tea comes out. Leave the cup upside down for a moment while you rotate it three times. Then turn the cup upright making sure the handle is pointed south.

Tea leaves should be stuck to the cup. There should be a variety of clusters and shapes that will have insights and answers. The reading usually starts from the rim of the cup and moves inward to the center.

The leaves near the rim are what is thought to happen
first and symbols near the center the distant future.

Tea leaf readings focus on positive energy rather
than negative. This could help you see everything that
might happen in the future in a positive light. It's
important to remember that not every cluster or shape
needs to be interpreted. Only the symbols that are
related to the querent's inquiry or question need to be
looked at.

Because there are over 150 regular symbols a book
like "Reading Tea Leaves" can be a helpful resource.

Here are some of the most common symbols.
Animals, mythical beings, objects, letters and
numbers. Some will be obvious like the following.

Angels – good news is coming

Circle – love or wedding

Crescent Moon – changes are coming

Cross – blockage or trouble ahead

Bird - travel or freedom

Waves – unity of some kind

Star – good luck is coming

Spiral – creativity is high

The handle of the cup is very important. It is the
energy conduit connecting the physical and the
abstract realms. The handle should point south.
That is where the querent should also be sitting facing

the handle. This position is to help signify the current environment. (In astrology the fourth house rules the home and family and is located in this position.)

If there are tea leaves near the handle of the cup that usually suggests events relating to the immediate surroundings. The further away from the handle symbolizes outside influences that might come in to make an event.

As you can see, reading tea leaves is a study combined with a gift. It could take years of practice, study and work to really get good at it. Remember any tool used in fortune telling needs to have an expert working it. An expert will have a higher level of understanding and have more experience to report a good reading. Also remember that a bad or untrue reading could ruin a person's life if they believe you.

Ouija Boards

The inventor of the Ouija board said he got the name from an ancient Egyptian word that means "good luck".

In 1891 the board was advertised as a talking board that could answer questions "about the past, present and future with marvelous accuracy." It promised a link "between the known and unknown". It sold for $1.50.

The Ouija board is a flat board with letters arranged in two semicircles across the board. There are numbers on it from 0-9. In the upper corners are the words "yes" and "no". At the bottom of the board the words "good bye" are printed in large letters.

There is a "planchette" teardrop-shaped device with a small window in the body of it. This is designed to move easily across the face of the board to spell out words or give messages. The whole concept of the game is that two or more people will sit around the board, placing their fingers on the planchette. Then a question is asked and the planchette is supposed to move from letter to letter spelling out the answer.

The numbers are used in many answers and the "yes" and "no" are for simple answers. The board's inventor thought of everything.

The invention of the Ouija board was one of the many that came out of the American 19th century obsession with spiritualism. That movement had the belief that the dead could communicate with the living.

Spiritualism had been raging in Europe for years before it hit America in 1848. The Fox sisters were the first to really open up this way of thinking. The Fox sisters claimed they could receive messages from the dead by asking them to tap or rap the answers on the walls to their questions.

This started the movement of channeling in parlors. With all the attention these sisters and others received through national press, spiritualism reached millions at its peak in the second half of the 19th century.

Around 1862 so many people were dying in the Civil War that the spiritualism movement grew to unheard of numbers. People were desperate to connect with their loved ones, especially the ones that had gone off to war and never returned. Less than thirty years later the Ouija board was on the market and selling as fast as they could stock the shelves. Because many people wanted to connect to the dead there had to be a better and faster way than taps on the walls.

The board was marketed both as a mystical oracle and a family entertainment game. Back in those days communicating with the dead was viewed as normal by much of the American population. It wasn't viewed as weird or strange. Today it is looked down on or people see it as talking to the devil, going against God or being processed.

The truth is the first producer of the board, Kennard Novelty Co., wasn't thinking about any of this. They just wanted to put out a game out that would let people think they could connect with their dead loved ones in their own parlor while they were making money.

The makers of the board knew that getting an appointment with a spiritualist was getting harder and harder and the price of those readings was growing. The board presented a way people could talk to their dead family members or friends without having to wait or even pay for an appointment with a medium. They could get messages quickly and safely in their own parlors. The Ouija board gave ordinary people control of talking to the dead. It was a great success and the "talking board" was born.

However, most scientists agree that there is nothing mysterious about the board. There is a psychological event known as "emotional contagion". When someone is feeling fear or "creeped out", they can pass that feeling on to other people who are near them. This condition can travel through a whole group of people.

This condition can cause hands to shake or tremble which may make it look as if the planchette is moving across the board on its own. This can convince everyone that something from another world is moving the device. Everyone in the room can believe something is happening when it's not. Now if the planchette moves on its own when no one is touching it, then you know a spirit moved it.

The board has been popular for over 120 years and it was accepted as a fun thing to use but that all changed in 1973 when the movie "The Exorcist" came out. The movie showed a young girl being possessed by a demon after playing with a Ouija board. The movie scared the hell out of people and made them believe the board was now evil and filled with demons and other dark monsters.

Before that movie the board was looked at as a source of entertainment. In 1951 the I Love Lucy show featured Lucy and Ethel in a séance and the board was depicted as a joke and silly. In a matter of a few years the Ouija board went from a family game and entertainment to a spiritual tool to talk to the dead and then to an evil board that can bring forward demons.

So how does the Ouija board really work? Scientists say the board is powered by a principle known as the idiometer effect. This is automatic muscular movements that happen without the conscious will or actual knowing it's happening to a person.

Dr. Chris French, professor of psychology and anomalistic psychology at Goldsmiths, University of London explained, "The thing about Ouija boards, downing rods, pendulums and other devises can be affected by a very small muscular movement that can cause quite a large effect. And with the Ouija board you've got the whole social context. It's usually used with a group of people and everyone has a slight influence. With the Ouija, individuals give up some conscious control to participate so they can say – it can't be me and no one person will take credit for the planchette' s movements making it seem like the answers must be coming from an otherworldly source. Moreover, in most situations, there is an expectation or suggestion that the board is somehow mystical or magical. Once the idea has been implanted in the mind, there's almost a readiness for it to happen."

With all that said, it doesn't mean you can't get messages from the board. Many times our subconscious knows the answer before our brain does and will unconsciously make our muscles move.

There is some evidence that when people are in a fearful situation they can attract dark energies or entities. Demons and dark spirits feed on fear and that is an opening for them to come to you. So if you use the board with the intent to talk to loved one on the other side, you still need to protect yourself from dark energies. If your intention is to communicate with demons and dark energies through the board then the changes are high that you will communicate with these types of energies.

So just like many of the other tools used to talk to spirits, fortune tell and get other messages, it's going to depend on who's working it, their mindset and the location. However, a word to the wise – Ouija boards are probably not just a toy and never have been.

Chinese Fortune Sticks

Ancient China is known for its mysticism and fortune telling. This talent goes back to the Jin Dynasty about 266-420 CE.

The Chinese fortune sticks started in temples. Back then the Chinese really believed that fortune tellers, who were mostly monks, were able to see into the future and tell them what was going to happen to them.   Many temples still use this means of fortune telling today.

The main purpose back then was to calm and unburden people lives. The fortunes where mostly focused on positive issues and problems so that people would feel there was always hope. When this practice first started, the people believed that the sticks were part of the gods and the divine.

In today's world the fortune sticks are still important and very much believed in. However, some view it as something fun to do just for the sake of tradition. This tradition has spread worldwide and anyone and everyone can do it, you don't need to be a monk or priest but it can be helpful.

The original name for the sticks was Kau Cim. Here are two components you have to have to be able to use and read the sticks.

1. The cim tong or cim bucket
2. The sticks or cim – there are usually 100 sticks painted red at one end. Each stick has a number on it and no numbers are repeated.

One way to 'read" the sticks is described below.

The querent, the person being read, should think or ask a question and not change it in the middle of the reading. The cup or cim tong is shaken and tipped slightly downward. This will help one of the sticks to slide out. If more than one stick falls out of the cup, the reading will not count and the querent must start over.

When only one stick falls out, you write down the number that is displayed on it. Typically the number will relate to a Chinese Jueju poem. The poem is believed to be the answer from the deities just for the querent.

(Jueju (绝句) is a style of jintishi, or "Modern shi **poetry**", that grew popular among **Chinese** poets in the fifth to sixth centuries in the Tang Dynasty. **Jueju poems** are always quatrains, with each line consisting of five or seven syllables each.)

Usually the answer will need to be interpreted by a specialist who is generally a Taoist monk or a fortune teller. The specialist will use a book of Chinese stories and poetic poems. The accuracy of the answer will depend heavily on the interpreter. Most people will consult several different specialists to see if they get similar interpretations which will prove to be the correct answer.

There are several different versions of these sticks but all are based on the same practice.

Chi Chi sticks were introduced into the US in 1915. It used only 78 sticks and the oracles had different content and interpretations. These sticks became popular among African-Americans in the 1920's and 1930's. The sticks were exported from China through mail-order. However when Japan invaded China in WWII, the trade routes were disrupted. Because of this, the popularity in the US came to a quick halt.

Kau Cim was originally a Taoist practice that was changed and adapted to Buddhism. It is called Guan Vin Oracle. The interpretations have their emphasis on beliefs to fit the Buddhism religion.

This variation was adapted in many countries around the world. Each country seemed to have its own name for the sticks. Thailand called it Siam Si. There is a similar practice in Japan called O-Mikuji which is done with fortunes written on a piece of paper.

So if you are going to use this ancient way of telling a fortune or future, be prepared for different interpretations and it might get confusing.

Dowsing with a rod
&
Dowsing with a pendulum

Today we think of dowsing mainly to find water.
However dowsing is an ancient art that has been used
to find everything from water to gold and to answer
questions, tell the future and get messages from the
dead.

Dowsing is thought to have started 6000 to 8000
years ago. It was practiced widely on the Island Of
Crete in Greece as early at 400 BC.

Homer, a blind Greek poet, called dowsing
Rhabdomancy, which means 'Divining Rod' in Greek.
Back then, dowsing was used to tell the future or talk
to the dead with a pendulum.

In the 1400's dowsing was called "Virgula Devine"
which in Latin means "dowsing with a rod shape
tool." This was when dowsing for water and minerals
became popular. In Germany they called a forked
stick tool, "deuter", meaning "to show", "to indicate",
"to point out", or "to strike".

Christopher Bird, the author of "The Divining
Hand", states that no one is certain of the origin of

the verb to "dowse". It seemed to appear around
1650 in an essay by English Philosopher John Locke.
He wrote that by using a dowsing rod you could find
water and precious minerals such as gold, silver and
mineral ore.

Locke was the person who put together the phase –
Dowsing Rod. This phase was from a long dead
English language of Cornwall. The "dowsy" meant
Goddess and "rhod" meant tree branch and from that
he "coined" the phase, Dowsing Rod.

It's widely thought that people who are diviners,
dowsers, seers, mediums, clairvoyants and the like
have self-trained themselves, practiced and have a
profound knowledge of how the Universe works and
can bring forward hidden senses to know things
others don't.

The following is a definition of modern dowsing by
Raymond C. Willey. "Dowsing is the exercise of a
human faculty, which allows one to obtain
information in a manner beyond the scope and power
of the standard human physical senses of sight, sound,
touch and the such."

Another way of explaining it is when you are
dowsing you are searching for something whether it is
water or minerals or just answers to your questions.

Seems the most popular tool with water and mineral dowsing is a forked stick. It would look something like a Y.

When using this Y shaped tool, the V part of it are the handles. You should have one part in your right hand and the other in your left. The straight end of the stick should be pointing at the sky. As the diviner walks the ground, the straight part of the rod should point from the sky to the ground where there is water or minerals.

Here again science tries to debunk dowsing by saying that ground water exists under most of the Earth's surface. They point out that a diviner can't tell the depth of the water, quantity or quality of the water. However it's been my experience that you have to find the water before you can test it.

Because drilling is expensive you don't want to guess where there might or might not be water. Most dowsers practice in rural areas where wells are a must.

I wrote this chapter so everyone has some sense of dowsing and where it came from. Now we are going into a chapter about pendulums and how they can work for spiritual communication.

(The next chapter was written by Suzanne Gwen – a good friend and client. Because I don't use a pendulum, I wanted to include information from someone who does. I hope you enjoy it.)

Talking to Disembodied Spirits
With the Pendulum
By Suzanne Gwynn

I need to start out by saying I am not any kind of expert on the Pendulum. I have heard about them for many many years, but have not studied them, learned about them or tried them for most of my life. When the time was right for me to try out the Pendulum in order to get in contact with my
father, the only thing pushing me forward was the desire to communicate with him on "the other side".

I've been interested in spiritual things since age seven when I heard a voice in my head one morning while weeding a new ivy bed. The voice said I would always be "safe in the universe". This
voice seemingly came out of the blue. But it was a voice I needed to hear as I was a rather unhappy child living with an abusive mother who did not want me. Her remedy for my existence was to turn me into the family scapegoat.

I was given the feeling I was not well liked in the world and for some reason these voices were very comforting and warm. I have never forgotten that

first morning communication with whom I knew
not. But it felt very real and has sustained me through
many difficulties even until today.

  Although not a regular event in my life, when my
difficulties felt beyond my ability to cope,
signs came my way to remind me I was part of a
warm, safe universe and was not forgotten or alone
in the Cosmos. One sign was the shaking of the
Cascade Mountains right in front of me. Talk
about moving mountains, it wasn't me, but I knew
someone was out there trying to communicate with
me.

  So, other than this spirit world, my life felt pretty
ordinary and uneventful. I went to college, married,
had three children, got divorced, married again and
lived a life with no great excitement. At that time I
never saw or appreciated the depth of my "normal"
experiences. But the one thing I did was continue to
search for spiritual meaning in my life.

  I became very active in several different churches in
different states over the years and looked for
meaning where I couldn't find it for myself. Well, I
didn't find what I was looking for in one
single church. Oh yes, I met some very nice people
and made a few friends along the way but
found no answers to show me how to feel the

closeness to those voices and shaking mountains
with which I wanted to connect. Those were the few
experiences which met me at a depth inside my soul
where I felt loved.

  So a number of years ago I gave up searching the
church pews and pulpits for answers to satisfied
me. I started doing a lot of reading about what I refer
to as spirituality rather than religion. My
eyes opened a great deal and I was driven inside to
seek more of this larger world of the Cosmos
which was not trapped by rules and ritual and was
inclusive of all people and animals and nature and
even me. I was free to experiment and decide for
myself what felt warm and fuzzy and loving. The
same feeling I had at age seven returned and I realized
finally I was on a path which would work for me.

  I learned I could, through the help of a medium, find
people on the other side of the veil who knew of my
experiences and from their perspective were able to
make me feel loved and made me feel part of
something whole rather than a scapegoat who couldn't
fit into life on the Earth. The medium I found who
mixed best with my needs was Shirley, the author of
the book you now hold in your hands. She is
compassionate, and a generous, understanding person
who makes you feel you are her only client.

I worked with Shirley several years talking with my
father with whom I was close to on the Earth
side of the veil. Eventually I talked to other family
members and learned to have more love for
myself and realized my mother had her own lessons to
learn and from her current perspective she is
very loving. We were finally able to forgive each
other.

The Earth seems to be our school house and
sometimes we need to connect with the other side to
grasp more difficult lessons.

So, on to the pendulum: I have not been able to
master the art of telepathic communication in the
form of complex conversations with my family and
the spirits. As much as I would like to have that gift it
escapes me. So I, in a rather arbitrary manner,
decided I would try to talk with my father via the
pendulum.

I did not read any books. I did not attend any
classes or ask anyone how to use this tool. I went on
line and picked out a few attractive pendulums and
bought them. I bought what appealed to me
visually. I considered nothing else. Some were more
fun than others to use for no apparent reason except
how they felt in my hand. I finally just settled on the
one I liked the best and now use only that one.

Well, it worked! I was able to get yes and no answers
from my father immediately.   At first I didn't know
whether or not I was getting the right answers. I
would write down my questions and check them out
with my dad when I was talking through Shirley.

It seemed too easy but my answers were generally
correct. So as time went on I gained confidence
in my pendulum skills. I started talking to other
passed family members with equal success. I can't
explain it. I have no idea how this works. I think it
has something to do with the energy
between us, but I don't know how we are connected
this way. What I do know is that it does work and I
receive great peace and joy from the connection.

As time went on, I learned to be more sensitive to
the feel of the pendulum. That is, I learned to
differentiate between different levels of involvement
my dad had in the answer. If he was
very enthused in perhaps my understanding of
something the pendulum would move with more
energy and make a wider sweep. Sometimes the
pendulum actually feels a bit heavier than at other
times.

I can interpret the meaning at the time it happens
but it is something only I can sense. Some things my
family, and spirits have learned together. Circles

started being part of the pendulum movement. Those generally mean we need to talk through Shirley because the subject is too complicated for the pendulum.

In time different family members have figured out how to create their own sweep. For example they might have their own angle rather than sweeping straight up and down. Sometimes if there is nothing to say the pendulum will just hang without any movement. I've also learned to get more complex questions answered by how I phrase the question.

So, there you have it! Why am I connected to this tool? I don't know. Perhaps it started at age seven for me. The Universe is clearly interested in talking with me and helping me. Some people have far larger capacity to communicate with the spirits on the other side of this veil, but this is what I experience. There are times I hear a voice outside of the pendulum like in my childhood experience, but generally my pendulum is my only telephone. I am extremely grateful for it.

I have learned our school yard and the whole Cosmos are connected. The school yard lessons are the hardest to understand as my many pendulum conversations have shown. But for some reason I

have been honored to be given the magic and love
behind a little round stone ball on a chain.

Muscle Testing

Muscle testing was first introduced and used in the early 20th century. It was to test the strength of polio victims. In 1949 two physiotherapists, Kendall and Kendall, started testing for other neuromusculoskeletal conditions.

Muscle testing does not work for future predicting or fortune telling. Your muscles cannot accurately give you an answer as to how things will feel in the future. It is meant to be used in the present moment and usually for a "yes" or "no" question. However it can help you realize how you feel about future options or choices.

I'm putting this practice in the book because it's another way to get quick answers to quick questions that many people use today. It's a simple concept that is more difficult to implement than most people expect.

With the right training and practice, it can help you identify what gives you strength and what weaknesses you have. Muscle testing can bring to the surface beliefs that you might not be aware of. Many people use muscle testing to ask about goals and better jobs or health.

Accuracy depends on "getting out of you own way". What this means is you have to have an open mind and not think about "how you want the outcome be". If you are vested in the outcome, it will put up a block to what is "actual" and what you want to be actual. If you really want an answer to be "yes", you will make that answer happen whether it's the truth or not.

The test can give you information from your subconscious but you can fool yourself if you aren't careful.

The statements or questions should be something like the following. "I am okay with making $90,000 a year." Then muscle test for a yes or no. Do not ask – "Will I make $90,000 this year?"

The next chapter is written by Wendie Kause. She uses muscle testing and can explain how it works. Since I don't use muscle testing very much, I asked Wendie to explain how you might use it for yourself. (To find out more about Wendie, I have included her bio at the end of book along with mine. And she did write one other chapter in this book – Animal Medicine Cards.)

Muscle Testing

By Wendie Kause

Connection to Universal Energy through Applied
Kinesiology

I believe the best way to introduce you to the benefits
of Muscle Testing and its simple practice is to first
remind you that as in my last chapter about Animal
Cards, Muscle Testing has the same relationship with
the universal energy and the Mystery.

Muscle Testing simply put is the art of applying
pressure to a muscle in the body to get a specific yes
or no answer. It is most often utilized to verify if a
type of food, medicine, vitamin, or medical treatment
is in alignment or the best choice. However, it can
address many other aspects of our lives, relationships,
mindsets, personal development, and decision
making… even knowing if something is true.

The exciting news about Muscle Testing is that it is
not only widely used in alternative medicine practices
and spiritual communities. It is extensively accepted
by linear sciences as well. That is because it is a
measurable and provable science.

I am eternally grateful that science, physics, and
quantum physics, align with metaphysics and many of
its practices, like Muscle Testing and Energy Work.

Before I dive too deeply into the history and how it works. I want to refer you to a couple of authors who have provided concentrated scientific reports, clinical studies, and graphs and charts to back up each occurrence. If you like to read research papers and dive into numbers and measurements, please read either of these authors. They will not only provide all the scientific data you could want but also share an in-depth and practical methodology of muscle testing.

David R. Hawkins, M.D., Ph.D., Power vs. Force, The Hidden Determinants of Human Behavior and Dr. Joe Dispenza, Becoming Supernatural, How Common People Are Doing the Uncommon. They have over 20 years of clinical studies and research, involving millions of collaborations and test subjects.

What's to follow is a much-abridged history and a bit of practical application based on my personal experience. The goal is to give you a taste of the benefits and enough information to get you started. Finding out for yourself how accurate it is. I promise you; you won't go away disappointed when you try it!

In 1971 Three physiotherapists published a definitive study on Muscle Testing. They discovered that.

1. The strength and weakness of every muscle were connected to the health or pathology of a specific corresponding body organ, much like the ancient acupuncture meridians.

2. They demonstrated that muscles instantly became weak when the body was exposed to harmful stimuli, either physical or mental/emotional. While substances or emotions that were therapeutic to the body made the muscle instantly stronger.

Since then, Applied or Behavioral Kinesiology (Muscle Testing) has become more and more mainstream. Study and new applications continue to this day.

How it Works

One of the best things about Muscle Testing is that the body will respond accordingly. Even if the subject has no idea what was being tested or how Muscle Testing works.

There are a variety of ways Muscle Testing can be done. It was first developed as a two-person process, but over the years, solo techniques have been established. Both are just as accurate, but I find it takes a bit of practice to interpret my own Muscle Testing measurement. I will first describe the standard two-person technique.

The person being tested stands or sits and holds out an arm. It does not matter which arm; However, most people automatically hold out their dominant arm. The tester tells the subject to resist while taking two fingers, placed on the wrist of the arm being held out. Then pushes down firmly. This determines the base pressure between the subject and the tester.

A statement is then made by either party while the subject holds it in their mind. The tester then applies pressure again. If the statement is Negative or False, the test subjects' muscles will go weak. If the statement is positive or yes, the test subjects' muscles will go strong.

This technique can be used to evaluate health-related items, as mentioned before. Or it can be used to assess a company, which movie you should pick, whether or not an individual is a good match, or even the truth of something. It cannot, however, be used to foretell the future.

Maybe someday it will, but there is not enough data to back it up. As I have said, energy does not have a beginning, it never ends and cannot be destroyed. I definitely believe that it can assist in predicting the future relative to our current timeline. But, studies have not been thoroughly conducted at this time, at least not that I am aware of. And since clinical studies, creating reports, and records are not in my wheelhouse, I sure will not be the one to perform that research. I'm happy to wait.

Because Muscle Testing is so simple, many have a hard time believing the validity of the technique. I suggest that you try it yourself. You may have to work on several subjects covering a variety of topics to be fully convinced. But I can tell you for nearly 20 years of using it myself, it has always been 100% accurate.

Another two-person technique that is often used is to have the subject stand. The tester asks the subject, "Show me a Positive or Yes." The subject automatically leans either slightly forward or slightly back. The tester than asks, "Show me

if the product is usually a good choice for most, it may not be Negative or No." Again, the subject will lean forward or back a bit. This establishes the muscle reaction. Once the Positive/Negative muscle response is determined, the tester will make statements or ask questions, just as in the two-finger technique described above.

Muscle Testing can also be done alone. I must admit, I find it more challenging to determine the base with my own body. But like anything else, a bit of practice provides excellent results.

As with the two-person technique, you must first establish the base strength and weakness before inquiry. Energy levels and base strengths vary depending on health, temperature, and mindset. Make sure to confirm your base each time you do muscle testing.

Take your thumb and index, middle or ring finger, and press them together. Many people find that the ring finger is the best to use, as it is the weakest finger, therefore the easiest to measure the pressure. I personally like the middle finger because my thumb and ring finger do not want to cooperate, and it is hard to reach my ring finger with my thumb. It really makes no difference on which finger you use. Once you have decided which finger works best for you, I recommend that you always use it. You will need to practice reading your own muscle reactions.

Now that you have chosen the finger that works best for you press them together. Take the index finger of the opposite hand and insert it between the thumb and finger. Establish your base pressure, just as you did with the two-person technique. Now use the index finger to break the hold. Pay attention to how difficult or how much force it took to break the thumb and finger apart. Now make a negative statement and break. Then break after making a positive statement. You can do this several times to discern your own measurement.

The best way to ask the questions is to make sure that they are simple, concise yes or no questions. You cannot ask questions like, "How does it make you feel?" It must be framed; "Vitamin D is a benefit to my (your) body." Or "Is Vitamin D a benefit to my (your) body?" "It is a good idea to go on a date with Joe?" Or "Should I rent "It's A Wonderful Life?"

As you can see, it may take you a bit to determine the strength of Yes and No answers relative to the outcome. In this example, "Should I rent "Its a Wonderful Life" movie?" You can not ask and either or question together. You have to first ask, "Should I rent "Its a Wonderful Life"? Measure the response. Then ask about the movie "Die Hard" It's very possible to get a YES answer to both questions. Yup,

from there, you will need to make your own choice
without assistance. Or you could ask a more specific
question. "Will watching Die Hard be a positive
influence on my evening?" Do you see where I'm
going with this? To get more specific answers, you will
need to ask more specific questions.

Try this the next time you're at a grocery store. Stand
in front of cookies, candy, or some other not so
healthy snack item. Ask your question. "Does this
cookie provide health benefits to me?"? Then move
over to the organic vegetable aisle. Ask, "Does this
carrot provide health benefits to my body?" You can
do this out of your own cupboard or medicine cabinet
too.

Determining what items are best for your body and
what may not be so good for you is a fabulous asset.
Can you see how you may be able to confirm what
you may be allergic to or not? Even if the product is
usually a good choice for most, it may not be the right
choice for you. There are people allergic to
strawberries, glutton, and any number of things.

Next time you are trying to choose between two
brands of vitamins, as an example. You will be able to
utilize muscle testing to determine which one is best
for you.

Can you tell I am offering uses of Muscle Testing
from the profound to the inane? That's because the
more inane questions, like what I should watch and
what book I should read, are excellent practices for

following your intuition. Besides, whoever said that spiritual practice had to be purely sacred, forgets that humor and entertainment are part of the experience we each have on this relative plane of existence.

How I Use Muscle Testing

When I was in my 30's, I began to take a regular vitamin regimen. I soon discovered that my body was not responding well to it. I began to break out in boils in places I don't even want to talk about. I was working with a Certified Herbalist, and she assured me her products were of the highest quality. We mixed and matched for several months trying to determine precisely which vitamin was causing me so much trouble.

Then I remembered Muscle Testing. We found the brand that caused the problem. We replaced it with another, and I never broke out again. The funny thing was that the contents of the brand were basically the same as the brand we replaced it with. I can only guess it was the milligrams and the way it was blended that cause the issue. I do not know to this day. But what I do know is that I absolutely never add a new vitamin to my regiment without first muscle testing and have never had problems again.

I was so pleased when my Chiropractor asked permission to use Muscle Testing on me. I felt like I found a kindred spirit. She used the standing two-person technique to discover if my body needed more vitamin D and at what level. When that worked so well, I asked her to help me see if there was a more natural product I could use to replace my Synthroid, Thyroid replacement therapy. Through muscle testing, we discovered I was not a candidate for more natural supplements, but that my thyroid was basically dead, and I would need to take Synthroid or some variation indefinitely. For my own confirmation and peace of mind, I went to the doctor and got a blood test. I could have saved my money because the blood test confirmed her diagnosis using Muscle Testing.

A fun way I use Muscle Testing is in choosing books, movies, or restaurants I am not familiar with. It's so exciting every time I use Muscle Testing to select a restaurant when I am out of town. I often receive confirmation that I am on the right track by taking a peek at Trip Advisor or Yelp. Not once has my result differed from the overall reviews of the restaurant. Over time, I have come to trust my muscle testing completely.

Another compelling way I use muscle Testing, which is actually a combination of my innate intuition and Muscle Testing. Is to very accurately tell when someone is lying to me. Most of us can do this, too, if we pay attention to the signals in the form of energy and body language. Muscle Testing is a powerful way to verify if you suspect someone is lying. What you do with that knowledge is the question.

Using Muscle Testing

While Muscle testing may be able to help you know if someone is lying by asking the positive/negative questions. I caution you to use this information for its highest good. This information can lead to some pretty awkward situations otherwise. First of all, how would you approach the subject? By accusing someone of lying, how would it change or improve the situation?

Muscle Testing does not reveal the details of why a person is lying or precisely what they are lying about. To achieve this, you would have to ask very specific positive or negative questions. I would suggest, if you become aware that someone is not telling the truth, just keep it to yourself. Just as when you have "gut" feeling that someone may be lying to you, the only way to verify is to ask questions. Be kind, do not accuse. The untruth could be coming from many different areas in that person's life. It may not have anything to do with you.

Suppose you are using Muscle Testing in your coaching or therapy practice. In that case, you will need to dive deeper into the process than what you are getting from reading this basic introduction to Muscle Testing.

I would also advise when using Muscle Testing to remember that it is an extension of your or your subject's own energy that makes this work.

I attended training years ago. The teacher openly used Muscle Testing to call on individuals in the crowd, either for questions or give-a-ways. He stood up there, asking, "Is this the section I should choose from?" then he would choose a section and break it down further to an individual. I found this so distasteful. By doing this, he claimed that "He" did not make the choices, the Muscle Testing did. It was like he was trying to hide behind it and not take responsibility for choosing specific individuals.

While I believe that Muscle Testing did help him decide. The way he presented it took away ownership of his decisions. It was like he said, "Don't blame me, I wasn't the one who didn't choose you, the Universe chose for me." Again, we are all part of the Universal Energy, not separate from it. Do not hide behind the tool to not take responsibility for it.

With that said, Muscle Testing is a powerful tool to assist you in getting and staying in tune with your energetic universal knowledge. It is one of the most accessible and most accurate tools that you can use to do so. And it's Free! No products to be purchase or devices to carry around. I bet if you looked around, you could pay for schooling to fine-tune your ability to read and measure responses. But other than that, honestly, a good trip around YouTube will provide plenty of instruction for you to use Muscle Testing for yourself. Using it for medical or emotional treatment on others? Well, I would suggest that you practice, learn more, and become an expert before diving into that end of the pool. But in the meantime, you will be

blown away by how accurate it is, and as long as you
let folks know that you are new to this and they are
part of your learning process, go for it, give it you're
all! You can really make a difference in someone's life,
not to mention your own.

As with all these types of tools, Never forget, you are
the Creator. Never give your power away to anyone or
anything else. You are part of the Energetic Universal
Mystery.

Runes

The first runes were large stones used in towns to announce events or laws to the public, almost like our billboards of today. From the first discovery of runes it was obvious that the runic alphabet was not a 'one on one' with any one language. It seemed to have various contexts of multiple German languages. The shapes of the runes varied in the layout, usage, regional, social and other chronological differences. There was not anything that looked like a standardized runic alphabet.

The first organized rune alphabet was known as the Elder Futhark. This was a Scandinavian language which was set in place and used from 160 CE and ran into the Viking age. It was in use well into the 5th century.

There is a theory that this runic alphabet was developed by the Goths. They were a Germanic people that developed the Etruscan alphabet of Northern Italy. It was influenced by the Daten alphabet in the 1st and 2nd century.

Back then, runes were used as a written code and believed to have magical powers. They were often

used as magical charms for protection and healing.
They were also used to put a curse on someone.

Runes were used in England from the 5th century CE
until the turn of the 11th century CE. The
Scandinavians used them well into the Middle Ages
and beyond.

The first runes were craved into wood and soft
mental in the Viking age and these were erected
throughout Scandinavia. They are the only known
written contemporary during this period. Runes have
been found in Germanic speaking people from
Iceland to Scandinavia and throughout Central
Europe. Basically they were found anywhere
Germanic speaking people lived and everywhere the
Vikings touched.

Each rune is made up of vertical lines, usually one or
two with branches of lines that jut out diagonally,
sometimes horizontally, upwards, downward or
curved. They can be written and read from both left
to right and right to left.

There are major and minor versions and each rune
has a sound that is a name and a noun that is
associated with it. As you can see, there are still many
regional and temporal variations.

There is a lot of mystery around how the runes really
came to be but they have always been thought of as

being attached to magic or the gods. Norse
mythology offers that the god Odin gained the
knowledge of the runes after he stayed hanging in the
"windy tree" without food or water for nine nights.

When the rune language was invented, it was used
for communication mainly for the living. Now they
are used to answer life's questions and talk to souls
who have crossed.

The word "rune" means mystery, whisper or secret.
The rune practice today usually has 30 runes and is
known as the Anglo-Saxon Futhore.

They have gone from large tablets to small tiles that
are stored in a bag. There are several lay outs you can
do, much like Tarot card lay outs. There is a book
that comes with the tiles so you know what each tile
means. There is also a definition for each of the
pictures on the tiles to help divine the reading.

Each rune has a letter of this language as well as a
symbol and each are used in translating answers of
questions you might ask.

Whatever you are using the runes for, the questions
or intent needs to be clear in your mind. It's not
about seeing the future; it's about looking for the
possible causes of the issue, the effects from it and
then seeing the potential outcome.

How to use dreams

There are all kinds of dreams but the ones that might be able to tell you the future are called "precognitive dreams". However, if you want to see the information in these dreams you first have to remember them. Then you will need to identify their symbols, analyze the content and understand the limits of dream interpretation.

To help you remember your dreams, put a tablet and pen or pencil next to your bed on your bed stand. Each night before you go to sleep, pick them up and say, "I will remember my dreams." Then put them down. Do this three times in a row each night just before you close your eyes.

This exercise will put a command into your subconscious. Because our subconscious never sleeps, it will start to remember your command and your dreams.

When you wake up, lay there for a few moments with your eyes closed. Think only about your dreams. Try to recall as many details as you can, colors, people, images and/or places. Try to figure out where you were in your dream and who was with you. Then grab the tablet and write it all down before you get out of bed. And even in the middle of the night if you wake up.

What happens when you start to wake up, you start to move. This movement makes your brain wake up and it starts to check your body to make sure it's okay. It will do a systems check – the heart is beating, the lungs are getting air, the mouth is starting to move and all the other things your body does when it starts to wake up. All of this will make you forget your dreams.

Reading dreams can be a lot of work but they can give you a lot of information if the interpretation is correct. Dreams can inform you about where you are and what might be happening in your spiritual, emotional and even physical world.

You need to see if the dream was or seemed to be in the past, present or future. Did you recognize the place or the people in your dreams? What kind of mood were you in when you went to bed? What were you thinking about just before bed? All of these things can have a big effect on your dreams.

The following is an example of a precognitive dream that I had many years ago. But because it came true, I have never forgotten it.

I was nervous about a trip I was going to take. It had been on my mind for weeks then one night I had

a dream about the trip. I was in a condo where I had
a balcony I could stand on and look down on a sandy
beach and the ocean was just a few yards away. I saw
the palm trees and when I went back into the room, I
saw two queen size beds, the bathroom and all the
furniture. I even meant a couple of people in the
dream before I woke up.

A few weeks later I was on this planned trip. When I
got there, it was déjà vu. The condo where I was
staying was just like my dream with the view of the
beach, ocean and the furniture. Even the two people
I had meant in the dream were there. I knew I had
traveled there in my dream and into the future.

When you are writing down your dreams, make sure
you put in all details even if you meet an alien.
Sometimes non-humans can mean a lot. There are
many symbols in dreams and we need to find out
what they symbolize before we jump to a conclusion.
We can't always say that if we see "food" in our
dreams that it actually means "food". It could mean
we need to feed ourselves with better learning,
knowledge or spiritual thinking. So it's important to
look at all the dream not just a section of it.

Another example of what something can symbolize
is water. Water almost always represents your spirit or
spiritual life. If the water is frozen, you have stopped

moving in your spiritual life. If it's a fast moving river, you are moving fast in your spiritual life but be careful not to move too fast. If it's a peaceful lake, it means are in a good spot in your spiritual life.

Pay attention to the emotions of not only the person in your dreams but how you felt. Were you afraid, anxious, happy, sad, etc.?

To really be ready to interrupt your dreams, you should learn more about dreams and their general meaning. Because our daily lives can sneak into our dream world, you need to ask yourself how you are feeling about your life and your day.

There has been years of "dream studies" and there is a ton of information about dreams. Having a good dream dictionary is important in the interpretation of your dreams. This is also where your dream log becomes very useful.

After you have logged a few weeks of your dreams, you should be able to look at them and find a common cord or subject matter. Also, ask yourself if there are any objects or elements of your dreams that keep repeating themselves. This can help you understand what your subconscious is trying to tell you.

When you read your dream log, it will inform you what might be coming or what has already happened.

Remember that dreams are very personal and even if another person has a similar dream, the meaning can be totally different. This is why some scientists think a dream is just our brain firing off random visions, while others think it's a way our brain processes the stress of the day. Still others believe we are traveling out of our body to visit people, places and even into the future.

The fact is that analyzing your dreams could help you better understand yourself and your subconscious. Your dreams shouldn't run your life but should help you with messages and possible guidance for the future.

Sigmund Freud and Carl Jung were some of the first people that did in depth studies of dreams. They discovered just how much our subconscious can run both the wake time and sleep time. You might want to read up on their work. Carl even thought that our subconscious might pick up on a "collective unconscious" that moves across places and time.

And last but not least, be aware that there is no "one size fits all" when it comes to dreams. No one has all the answers. You are probably the best person to interrupt your own dreams.

Astrology

There are volumes of books written on astrology so we are only going to cover a very small amount of information and some of its history.

Astrology originated in Babylon about 2,400 years ago. About 300 years later it spread to the Eastern Mediterranean, then Egypt. The zodiacal signs originated in Babylon in the 1st millennium BC.

Back then people believed the movement of the planets and sun could tell the weather and how crops would do. They believed that the seasonal shifts were in conjunction with the celestial cycles and were signs from the gods. They also believed that the stars, planets and sun rotated around the Earth. But as we know now, the Earth is the planet that rotates around the sun.

There are drawings and carvings that show lunar cycles that were done as early as 25,000 years ago. Even back then, it was noted that high tides were somehow influenced by the moon. By the 3rd millennium BC, the awareness of the celestial cycles had grown. This is one of the reasons many temples and holy places were built in alignment to the raising of the sun, stars and moon which were believed to be linked to the gods.

Astrology really became popular in the US in the late 1880's. It was used by combining meanings of what the fortune teller thought and the alignment of the planets and what that meant to each individual person.

For example – If Saturn is in the first house of your chart it can mean something different than if it is in the first house for someone else. Saturn is the planet of restrictions so a reading around this situation might mean you will have more responsibility or even denied responsibility.

It could mean a cold person is coming your way or it's a good time to restrict food and go on a diet. It will all depend on the rest of the chart and what planet is in what house. An astrology reading can be a very long and drawn out process and leave you a little confused.

So looking for answers and predictions in the movement or placement of the celestial bodies really isn't science. It's all about repetition of how the Earth rotates. The cycles will repeat themselves over and over again because of the movement of Earth. Ancient Egyptians knew when Sirius, the Dog Planet, came around in mid-July the annual flooding of the Nile was near.

If you really watch the sky and chart the planets, you will see that patterns repeat themselves over and over again. This is also why travelers used the sky and stars as a compass. They knew that certain clusters of stars would always appear in the same place in the spring, summer, fall and winter. Once they knew that the Big Dipper was always in the Western sky in one of the seasons, they could use it as a guide to see which direction they were going.

When a planet goes Retrograde, it is appearing to go in a reverse direction to Earth. This is an optical illusion caused by differences in the Earth's orbit. Mercury is always the closest to Earth in its orbit. (Venus is the closest but on its orbit it will swing farther away from Earth that Mercury) That means Mercury will go Retrograde three to four times a year.

The frequency of this makes Mercury an ideal scapegoat for anything that goes wrong during this time period. I personally don't believe that this optical illusion can cause us bad luck. I believe that if we believe that, we will make our own bad luck.

This relates back to the belief that if you believe hard enough in anything, you can bring it to you whether it's good or bad.

So if you want a fast reading, astrology is probably not for you. It's an interesting study of the skies and like everything else it's all in what feels right to you about the information you get.

Lithomancy

Lithomancy is a psychic art and is known as "reading stone, divination by stones, gems or crystals." It is similar to reading runes, Tarot cards or tea leaves. It's casting or picking stones to tell the future or getting inside information on a specific subject or question.

This is an ancient art that is associated with both witchcraft and Shamanism. Because each stone is assigned a title and meaning, like Tarot cards, this is considered sorcery.

This method of a psychic reading offers insights into different issues. It can reveal how these issues interact and manifest on a daily and weekly basis.

Patterns in the stones will outline, in a symbolic form, present situation, upcoming situations, challenges, opportunities and other changes that might come into play.

They can reveal "the light at the end of the tunnel."

All this is like a psychic reading where there is hope and guides you to use your free will to empower yourself.

As you can imagine, no pattern is ever the same. This makes each reading as individual as a psychic reading. As the energy around people change with their thoughts, words, actions and choices the pattern of the stones will change.

The patterns can help get information about past lives, spirits guides, souls who have crossed and other issues. It is somewhat like Tarot cards where the interrupter needs some intuitive gift to help see what the symbols are telling the person who is being read.

An example would be when the 'death card' in a Tarot card turns up in a reading. It usually doesn't mean someone is going to die. It can mean the person is letting go of something so they can start something new. This letting go can be a person or a thing or even a way of life that needs to change so that they have room for a new person, thing or energy to come into their life. So it is the death of something old to make room for something new.

Most people are concerned with the present moment or immediate future. This is why we want to look at what might be coming in the future. The choices we make today will influence the future so it's good to have as much information as we can get so we can make wise choices now.

If we step back and look at our lives, we will see it's a sequence of events or actions that take place by own choices. We can start to see a pattern of good or bad choices and start to become aware of making wiser choices to better our lives.

There are several ways to "throw" stones to receive an answer to your questions. One of the easiest ways is to do a quick reading with a black stone and a white stone.

You can assign "yes" to the white stone and "no" to the black stone. You put them in a cup and while you gently shake them, you ask a "yes" or "no" question. Then you gently roll the stones out. The one that is closest to you will be your answer.

You can add a third stone with a different color and assign "maybe" to it. However, if that comes up, it really isn't much of an answer and you might want to go back to just the "yes or no" stones.

You can use as many stones as you want with each having their own assigned meaning. In the British Isles 13 stones are usually used. Seven of them represent astrological signs – the sun, the moon, Mars, Venus, Mercury, Jupiter and Saturn. The other six represent home, life, love, luck, magic and news. This way you can get more detailed information.

All the stones should be about the same size. You can find them on the beach or sidewalk or you can buy them at a gem shop. Look for different colored stones or ones that have curious markings on them.

Once you have selected your stones, it's time to read up on how to do a stone reading. They can get very complexed with more stones.

It's too difficult to write all the instructions here but before you start a reading, make sure you understand how the stones work. This can be a fun way to get answers to your questions. However like everything else, it takes practice, learning and studying to make sure you understand the symbols and meaning of the stones. The advice I can give you is to start off slow and simple until you really understand it.

The next chapter is written by Lynn Spicer who uses Shaman Stones to do readings. I think you find the information very interesting and informative. Her bio follows her story so you can learn more about her.

A LITTLE HISTORY OF SHAMAN STONES

By Lynn Spicer

The use of Shaman Stones dates back to prehistoric times, specifically the Neolithic period. Early man took refuge and lived in the caves shaped by rock formations. The caves provided shelter from the elements and the creatures that were higher up on the food chain and saw man as prey.

Stones witnessed the birth of plants, animals, trees and fish. Through all the ages they have watched man both suffer and thrive. They are referred to as "the grandfathers." Mankind stays connected to Mother Earth through plant spirits, energy healing, stone spirits, or prayer. We connect back to Earth and keep balance within the circle of life. Using stones is one of the oldest healing methods ever used, and it is still being used today.

Stones can be used for many things—spiritual purposes, healing, protection, connection, lucid dreaming, astral traveling, connecting to spirit guides, and grounding.

There are several stone structures today that are believed to harness energy: the great pyramids and Stonehenge are two such structures that we are familiar with. There are many more, but these are the most known.

Native Americans used stones in their sweat lodges for prayer and they asked for advice and wisdom. Water was ladled on them to produce steam and "the Grandfathers," would answer those that requested advice. Answers could come from either visions or signs from the Universe.

SEEKING YOUR SHAMAN STONES

Begin by asking yourself what is your heart's desire. Do you want to connect with spirit guides, both animal and angelic? Do you want to use them for healing purposes? You may have a different heart's desire than mine, but I wanted to connect with animal spirit guides for advice and healing. I was fortunate enough that a Native American spirit guide also stepped up to offer his services for healing.

After you have chosen your heart's desire, you can begin to gather your stones. You will start with 10 stones representing your heart's desire. You are definitely not limited to just 10 stones—I have 15 in my pouch. You may want to also get a pouch to hold your stones in. I started obtaining my stones first through a guided meditation during a Dream Quest Workshop offered by Janice Lynch, pastor at The Divine Fellowship Church in Richland, Washington.

We were asked to take special note of any animals that appeared during our meditation. My first three stones were Tiger, Giraffe, and Fish. Other animals may appear to you in dreams, or other meditations. I'll explain what each animal in my Shaman Pouch represents later in this chapter. After you have seen your animal guides, you will want to go out and find stones and/or rocks that seem to represent your guides. It was advised to not use crystals because they tend to shatter when in a pouch with harder stones. After you have found your rocks, they are no longer rocks, they become Shaman Stones. They are sacred stones and have a sacred purpose. If you find a rock later that you identify with more, you can always change it out. You will want to thank the old stone and release it from its duty.

Below is a list we gathered from our Dream quest workshop:

Significator: This rock symbolizes you. You might want to take a walk in nature and utilizing your energy, ask the Universe to show you which rock is willing to represent that energy for you. After you find it, you will want to wash and dry it, and then place it in your Shaman Stone pouch.

All Okay: Search for a light-colored rock that seems to say yes or go ahead. It will appear to be brighter or it will stand out to you. You can utilize your energy in this process and ask the rocks which one will be your All Okay. Just trust the process and it will present itself to you.

Stop: You are searching for a dark rock. As you walk repeat, "no, stop, not okay." The rock will present itself to you.

Animal Spirit Guide: These rocks represent the animals that came to you during meditation. Hold the energy of each animal in your heart as you walk around. You will be drawn to the rock(s) that chooses to represent your animal spirit guide(s). Again, trust the process.

Dragon: Your dragon stone represents decisiveness and focus. Hold the energy of this in your awareness as you seek the stone willing to assist in this energy for you.

Knight: Knight represents creativity and compassion. Hold the energy of this in your awareness as you seek the stone willing to assist in this energy for you.

Elf: Elf represents fun and adventure. Hold the energy of this in your awareness as you seek the stone willing to assist in this energy for you.

Wizard: Wizard represents data and information. Hold the energy of this in your awareness as you seek the stone willing to assist in this energy for you.

Now that you have identified all these rocks, they are no longer just rocks. They are sacred Shaman Stones. Honor them as having a sacred purpose and they will honor you by assisting you in your journey.

Over the years, I have found charms that represent some of my Shaman Stones. I have blessed the old stones and released them from duty and added these charms to my Shaman pouch. I have a dragon, a wizard hat, a jester, and a sword.

Other stones I have added to my pouch represent totem animals. Totem animals present themselves to you to reveal messages from the Universe. For example, I have had dragonflies, doves, crows, squirrels, deer, cats, dogs, and insects come forward with messages specifically for me. To honor them, I find stones with their energy and use them in my readings.

You may find it helpful to keep a list of your individual stones and what they represent to you. Use this list when doing readings with your stones. Eventually, you won't need to carry the list; the stones and their energy will become very familiar to you.

HOW TO DO A READING

I usually ask my client to hold the stones and charms in their hand(s). They then shake the stones and blow on them three times. As they blow on them, I ask them to seek their heart's desire or an answer to a situation they have questions about. After they blow their intention on the stones, they hold the stones about 6 inches up from my mat and drop them.

They cannot be just placed on the mat because the way they fall is relevant to their reading. I find the significator, and then all the stones closest to the significator reveal the answer to their question. The energy of these stones tells a story that gives them direction and guidance to their heart's desire. Stones outside the reading area have no information for the client so I just let them be.

MY STONES AND THEIR MEANINGS

The following is a list of the stones in my Shaman's pouch and what their energy represents to me:

SHAMAN STONES IN MY POUCH:

Tiger: Remain focused and patient. This animal spirit guide honors your healing and clairvoyant abilities. Stone—Tigers Eye

Giraffe: Keep your head up and don't be afraid to reach to achieve your goals. You have the gift of foresight and seeing signs. Stone—spotted agate

Fish: You can quickly adapt to life's circumstances. Also symbolic of intuition, faith, and sensitivity. People born with the fish spirit animal are independent and fierce. You feel better around water. Stone—fossilized tooth.

Spider: This stone is about creativity and the ability to weave words together. You are slow to anger, but have a sting when riled. Stone—round black obsidian

Goose: Be appreciative of all things life has brought to you. You are very nurturing and protective towards family. When an idea or thought is gifted to you, let it take flight. Stone—gray agate

Crow: You let yourself be guided by Spirit and signs from the Universe. Keep your eyes open for someone trying to trick you. Stone—flat black obsidian

Blue Jay: Pay attention to nonverbal clues that someone is trying to deceive you. You like to dabble in several things at one time and know a lot about many different subjects. Be careful not to come across as a know-it-all. Stone—holly blue agate

Buffalo: You will always have what you need. Focus on feeling grateful and appreciative. Stop feeling sorry for yourself and honor what you already have. Stone—Montana agate

Fox: Listen and hear, look and see, sense and feel. Trust your senses to guide you. Be wary of someone who's attempting to trick you in some way. Stone—small red cornelian agate

Dove: Express your love to as many people as possible in words and deeds, even in small yet significant ways. It's important to nurture yourself with loving care. A spiritual renewal is beginning that's a result of intense self-examination and challenges. Stone—flat gray river rock

Praying Mantis: Make prayer, meditation or contemplation part of your everyday ritual. Listen to your instincts as to when to move forward and when to retreat. Stone—green bloodstone

Cat: Listen to your intuitive guidance; it's most likely an ancestor who's one of your spirit guides trying to communicate with you. Trust in your own capabilities. Stone: flat, broken river rock

Arrowhead: This is from my Native American spirit guide. He provides assistance in healing. If he comes up in your reading, he is offering to assist you.

TOTEM ANIMALS AND CHARMS:

Cornelian Agate: the stone of balance and grounding. Your guardian angel is letting you know they have your back.

Dragonfly: Stone is clear agate. Be on the lookout for any lies, deceit, or illusion that are clouding a current situation or relationship. Dragonflies often represent the spirit(s) of loved ones that have passed. They are sending you a message. Look for signs. You may start to go through a major transformation, just enjoy the process.

Key: It is time to unlock your creativity and show your wisdom.

About the author of this chapter:

Lynn Spicer is a resident of the Tri-Cities and has
lived there for 35 years. She has certifications for
Tarot Master, Reiki Master, and Aromatouch. In both
her tarot and reiki practice she uses essential oils to
enhance the experience. When she uses essential oils
in tarot readings, those oils meant for the client will be
put together in a roller bottle blend that represents
them and they will take it home with them. During
Reiki, Lynn uses muscle testing to see which oil is
required to assist in healing. During Aromatouch, a
series of oils are applied to the spine, back and feet to
release stress, improve the immune system, relieve
pain, and restore the body to a state of homeostasis.

It was during a Dream Quest workshop led by Janice
Lynch at The Divine Fellowship in Richland,
Washington, that she found her passion for Shaman
Stones--she felt that they called to her. Since then she
and her Stones have morphed into one being. They
give accurate answers to those seeking advice in a
kind, gentle way through the animal spirit guides they
represent

Automatic Writing

Loosely defined, automatic writing is the idea that a soul who has crossed over to the other side wants to communicate with us. Many think this is a way souls can talk to anyone. Automatic writing became popular during the Spiritualist movement in the late 19th century in America. It is said that there were more than eight million followers of the Spiritualist movement by 1897.

Here again the influence of the Fox sisters spurred another way to get hold of the dead. The Fox sisters would communicate with dead people through "knocks and taps" on walls and floors. But many times this took time to get an answer or you might not even get an answer. If you did hear the knocks and taps, you might not understand what they meant. People were looking for a faster way of communicating with these souls.

This need to "talk faster" to dead people led to the birth of automatic writing just as it had with the Ouija Board. Science is quick to point out that there is no scientific proof supporting automatic writing. This isn't that strange as science rarely supports any metaphysical discipline which includes Tarot cards, pendulums, psychic readings and any other tool in this book. However, there are thousands of people that have tired it and still use it today.

Automatic writing can be done with pen and paper, typewriter and even computer.

With any form of psychic divination, the more you practice the more you'll learn and understand the messages you are receiving. When I first started my readings, one of my teachers told me to practice, practice and practice some more. You can never practice too much if you want to be good at anything. Fortune telling or talking to dead people is just like any other art you want to learn, it takes some kind of work and practice.

Automatic writing is thought to be channeling spirits without being possessed which made it very popular with Spiritualists back in the 19th Century. Being possessed was a very real fear back then and it is still a fear today. Dark spirits can come in and if you are open to them, they can possess you. This is why you need to read and learn how to protect yourself before you start playing around with any tools that are in this book. One quick way to protect yourself is to put a bubble of protection around your body so no negative or dark energies can enter your energy field.

Francisco Chico Xavier, a Brazilian medium, was probably one of the most prolific automatic writers. He started writing when he was in grade school and actually won an essay contest that he claimed was written by a spirit. Even though he never finished school, he wrote books that were scientifically and literary written beyond his abilities.

Automatic writing was an important part of the Surrealist movement. This movement was founded by a French writer and poet, Andri Breton in the1920's. The group included writers, poets and artists.

This movement was influenced by psychological theories that were concentrated on the subconscious and its function and influence on our consciousness.

The Surrealism groups believed in "pure psychic automatism - the dictation of thought in the absence of all control by reason, excluding any aesthetic or moral preoccupation".

The Surrealists would meet in groups and discuss how they could improve and prove the beliefs of their movement. They would also play various games that they thought were spiritual or mysterious. Automatic writing and automatic drawing were among the most popular of their games. They became very good at playing these games and then interrupted the meaning of the writings and pictures.

They would try to write as quickly as possible to remove conscious control over what was being written. If the flow of writing was interrupted, they would start over. Once something was written, it was manipulated and reiterated to make other compositions.

If you would like to try automatic writing, here are some suggestions you might want to use. Make sure all distractions are eliminated. That means kids, TV, phone or any other distraction.

Next you will need to clear your mind, like you are going into a meditation. You should be sitting where you are comfortable and have a pen in your hand and a few pieces of paper in front of you.

As you ground yourself and empty your mind, you can start writing. Many people will just start writing words or a sentence. Many times this will create an opening for a spirit to come through and you may feel like words are just "popping" into your head and your hand is writing them down.

Don't worry about staying in the lines or how it looks or even the spelling. Just write the words down as you either hear them or your hand writes them. The words may not even make sense until you are finished. You don't want to interrupt anything until the writing has stopped. Trying to make sense of it before you finish will distract the flow and you will probably lose the connection.

If you have trouble getting started, you might want to write down your question and then see what response you get. If the words you are writing don't seem to correspond to your question that's okay. There are times we will get answers to questions we haven't even asked yet – at least not out loud.

Keep writing until the words stop. For some people this might be ten minutes while others might write for hours. There is no right or wrong on how long a session should last. When the spirits are done, they are done and no more words will come through.

When you are finished, it's time to look at what you wrote. Look for word patterns or themes. When words are repeated it means that subject is important. Whatever seems to be repeated is what you need to look at. See what resonates with you and what doesn't and go in the direction you think is pulling at you.

An example would be if money or finances keep showing up, that probably means you need to look at what you are doing with your money. Look for names and if you don't know who they are, you might be getting messages for someone else or this might be a person that will be coming into your life.

You might even have drawn symbols or doodles that might not seem important until you start putting the message together. Many times these doodles will fill in a gap somewhere. Sometimes pictures are the best way to get an idea or thought across.

Your writings might be neat and organized but they could also be a mess and all over the page. It doesn't matter as long as you got it on paper. And sometimes you will start at the beginning but skip the middle and go right to the end for the message to make sense. Sometimes the middle is the first message. You might have to go back and forth to make sense of the writing. Don't judge the looks of it or how you have to read it.

Remember it will take practice to get good at the messages you are bringing through. You will also have to interrupt what was on the paper and try to make sense of it. This might be the hardest part of the whole exercise. Take your time and really try to get the true meaning of the messages that came through.

It's fun and can be quite exciting to see what a spirit might want to say to you. So, one of these rainy or boring days, sit down to a quiet session of automatic writing.

Palmistry

The origins of Palmistry date back to ancient China, Tibet, Persia and other Eurasian landmass countries. It is believed that a wise Hindu man, named Valmiki, was the first to write a book about palmistry.

The translation of the book to English was "the technique of Valmiki on male palmistry". From India it spread as far as Egypt and China. The link between China and Europe was set when a Greek philosopher, Anaxagoras, started practicing it. It is said that even Aristotle practiced the "magic" of palmistry and presented readings to Alexander the Great.

A famous quote from Aristotle is "lines are not written into the human hand without a reason".

During the Middle Ages, the Catholic Church forbid palm reading. They characterized it as a form of pagan superstition. It was also forbidden during the Renaissance period. This period was a dark period for anyone who practiced palm reading and the art was almost lost.

Palmistry started to gain popularity in the 19th Century again in Great Britain. When the Cheirological society was formed, it brought back the art of palmistry and the "magic" of the art started to grow again. The society was formed to prevent charlatans from abusing the practice. The Cheirological society was responsible for showing and teaching people across the world the real magic and meaning of palmistry.

They spread the word from country to country and continent to continent. By the mid 1900's palmistry was fully integrated into the American pop culture.

Palmistry is the art of analyzing the physical lines and other features of a hand to interpret personality characteristics and predict future happenings. Occult traditions believe that the palm is seen as a microcosm of the entire Universe and holds clues and answers to a person's life.

Back when birthdays and other special days were unavailable to use in a horoscope reading, mainly because they hadn't been recorded, palm reading was considered the best way to get the information they wanted or needed. Today palm reading is very popular and many people enjoy the experience and information they get from a reading.

There are hundreds of books that explain the lines in your hands. If you are interested in learning to read palms, I would suggest reading a few books on it and even finding a seasoned professional to give you a few lessons.

Like everything is this book, studying, practice and some psychic or intuitive gifts are really required to do good fortune telling. Remember that telling the future is taken very serious by many people and you can either help them or hurt them.   It should always have a positive twist to it too. The other very important thing to remember is that nothing is set in stone. God gave us free will and not even He will take that away from us.

To get into all the lines, hills, valleys and other signs your hand holds is too much for this short chapter. Just know that when you start to study palmistry, there is a lot to learn.

You will also have to remember that as our life changes, the lines change. Many people think that if you have just one palm reading, that's it for a life time. That's not true. You probably need to get one reading once a year to keep up on what your hands are trying to tell you.

With each choice we make, our life will change. These changes will change our energy, aura colors and the lines in our hands. The lines change to help us see that the choices we make in the present moment will change how the future looks.

The next chapter is written by a friend and client about reading the whole hand, which includes the palm, fingers, finger prints and all aspects of the hand. Unlike the changing lines in your hands, finger prints never change. She will explain how she "reads" hands and what it can tell you about yourself.

LIFE PURPOSE HAND READINGS

By Marcella Theeman

The art and science of hand reading to show you the way forward in life and love!

Why are you here in this lifetime? What are your gifts? How can you find relationship compatibility? What's holding you back in life? Are you on your Path? If you are looking for insight into questions like these, it's time for a Life Purpose Hand Reading.

The practice of reading hands (sometimes referred to as palmistry or chirology) to understand yourself and those in your life at a deeper level has been around for thousands of years. For most of that time it has been a highly respected discipline in many parts of the world. In Western cultures it went through a period of decline. The logical Western mind tended to see it as woo-woo or at least lacking in scientific basis. Today, it is being restored to its rightful place as a legitimate science for understanding human behavior. Like most modalities for self-understanding (hand reading, tarot, numerology, astrology, etc.), there are different schools of thought with regard to hand reading. This chapter will focus on an approach known as Life Purpose Hand Reading.

WHAT IS A LIFE PURPOSE HAND READING?

A Life Purpose Hand Reading is a powerful and complete system of self-awareness. It looks at and analyzes your fingerprint patterns, along with the lines, gift markings and other markings in your hands. By interpreting this information, you can come to a greater understanding of who you are, why you're here on planet Earth and what challenges you're likely to face in life.

HOW IS A LIFE PURPOSE HAND READING DIFFERENT FROM TRADITIONAL PALMISTRY?

There are three main differences. First, a LPHR places much emphasis on the information contained in your fingerprint patterns. Your fingerprints are important because they're formed 5 months before you're born and never change. The lines in your hands also contain important information, however during your lifetime their configurations can change or even disappear. Second, a LPHR provides deep understanding of your emotional, creative and vocational potentials, but does not predict when or whether certain events will occur. So, a reading will provide insight as to why you're here in this lifetime. It will not tell you when and where you will meet a tall, dark stranger or how many children you're destined to bring into the world. Third, a LPHR typically involves taking an inked print or a digital photo of your hand and fingerprints in addition to looking at your actual, physical hand.

WHY ARE YOUR FINGERPRINT PATTERNS IMPORTANT?

Formed 5 months before you're even born, your fingerprint patterns are uniquely yours and never change. Even identical twins do not have the same fingerprint markings. Your fingerprint patterns are an integral part of who you are at the very deepest level. They play an important part in a Life Purpose Hand Reading.

WHAT TYPE OF FINGERPRINT PATTERNS DO YOU HAVE?

Take a few minutes to examine your fingerprint patterns. Bright light and sometimes even a magnifying glass will make this easier. How do your print patterns compare to the ones below?

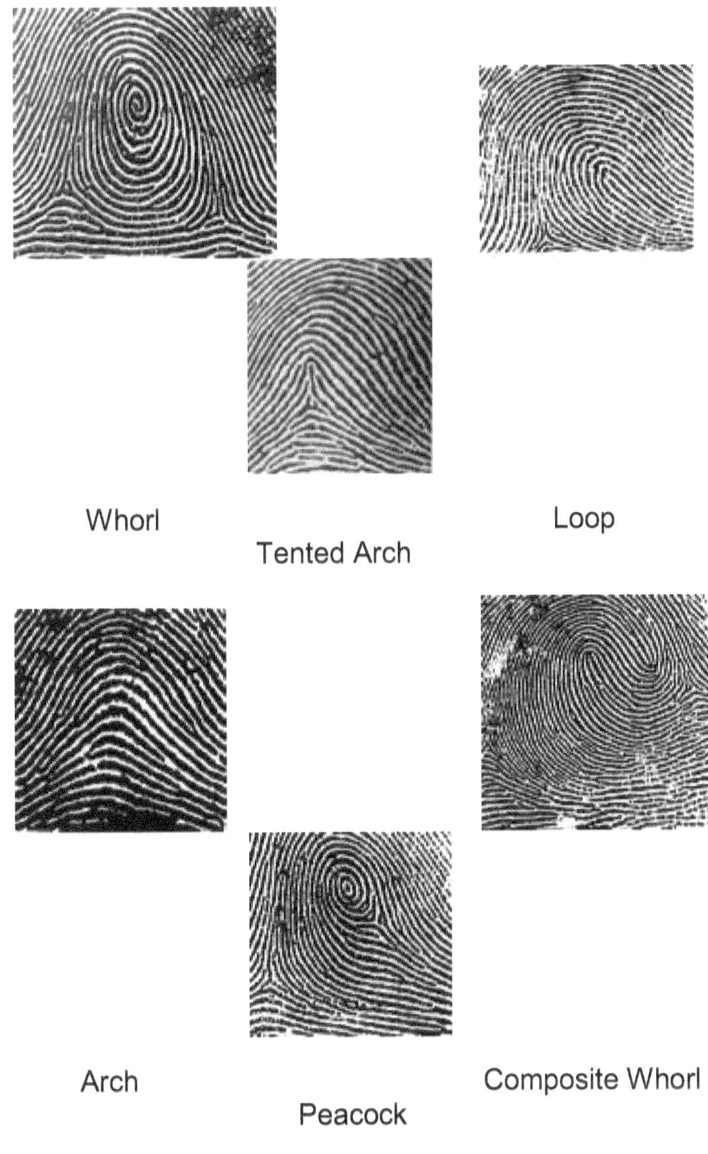

Whorl

Tented Arch

Loop

Arch

Peacock

Composite Whorl

SO, WHAT CAN WE LEARN FROM OUR FINGERPRINTS?

By examining your fingerprints you can determine your Life Purpose, Life Path and Life Lesson/Challenge. Your Life Purpose is your reason for being here in this lifetime. It may or may not be related to how you choose to make a living. A life on purpose seeks meaning. It's that place where life feels good and things really flow. By Life Path, we mean a recurring theme or energy in your life. Your Life Challenge or Lesson is your weak spot or shadow side. It's what gets in the way of living a fulfilling life.

For example, if you look at your fingerprints and find that 4 or more of them are whorls, your Life Path is to be of service by sharing wisdom and information. You are likely to be of an independent nature, highly intelligent and analytical. Owners of whorl-type fingerprints are typically private people who thrive on alone time. Not being able to share your wisdom and feeling confined or restrained are among your biggest fears.

Since this is an overview chapter, space and time do not allow for a complete explanation of each fingerprint type and its respective Life Purpose, Path and Challenge.

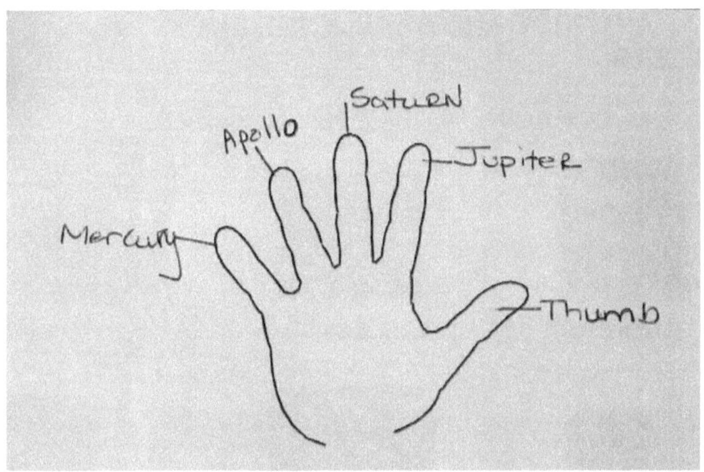

LOCATION, LOCATION, LOCATION

Not only is the type of fingerprint important, which finger it resides on needs to be taken into account. Each finger, as well as your thumb carries its own energy and potential for expression in the world. In hand reading, the energy each finger carries is associated with the name of a Greek god and the power they represent.

AREAS OF APTITUDE AND CHALLENGE IN OUR FINGERS

Before we talk about the energy/potential represented by each finger, let's talk about a few things to keep in mind while assessing the message they carry.

First, fingers represent your ***potential*** behaviors. Each finger represents certain qualities with both an upside and downside potential. For example, a certain finger might show a wonderful, high potential, but for whatever reason, you're not stepping up to it. Conversely, a finger might show a certain weakness but due to hard work and determination, you're overcoming that inherent weakness.

The **length** of a particular finger represents the amount of time/energy you spend in that area. A long finger = more tendency to spend time/energy; a short finger = less likely to spend time/energy in that area.

The **width** shows us how much of that quality you tend to display. A wide finger shows more of a particular quality whereas a narrow finger reveals less of a particular quality.

A finger's **posture** will indicate how strong or weak the traits of that finger are likely to be. A **strong** finger is solid, upright, and straight. A **weak** finger is bent, twisted and/or tilted.

To assess which of your fingers is strong vs. weak, conduct what's known as The Breakfast Test. Which finger(s) appear well-fed as opposed to needing to be beefed up.

In hand reading, the index or pointer finger is referred to as the **Jupiter** finger, named after the King of the Gods, Jupiter. Personality attributes for this finger when you are in balance are leadership, confidence, authority, vision and ambition. A balanced Jupiterian leader does what's best for the bigger vision of the entire realm. Too much Jupiter energy leads to a domineering, dictator type. Too little Jupiter energy is found in those who lack confidence or are overly timid. Typical Jupiter professions are CEO, Business Owner or Captain of the Team.

 The middle finger is named after Saturn, the God of the Harvest. Saturn represents the old traditions, rules and systems. Saturn energy strives to keep these systems in their place. It is all about rules, law and order, right and wrong. Balanced Saturn energy displays responsibility, discipline and attention to duty. Too much Saturn energy shows up as over responsibility. If you lack Saturn energy you tend to be irresponsible, run late for everything and/or have trouble meeting your basic needs. Typical Saturn professions are Agriculture, Education, Government, Research and Finance.

Next in line is the Apollo finger. Apollo is the god who drags the sun across the sky every day. The sun is a spotlight – it heats up and lights up our world. Apollonians (those with a lot of Apollo energy) need to be engaged in creative self-expression and then "light up the world" by sharing their creativity with others. Too much Apollo energy shows up as superficiality. Too little is displayed by those who are shy. Typical Apollo professions include The Arts, Drama, Fashion Design, Jewelers, Carpenters, Architects, and Software Developers. Hollywood is likely rampant with Apollo energy.

The pinky finger is represented by Mercury, the Messenger of the Gods. Mercury is the god of communication. Quick, sharp and clever along with excellent communication skills is the domain of Mercurians. Too much Mercury energy shows up as con men and manipulators. Those who have an inaccurate perception of self and others are displaying a lack of Mercury energy. Typical professions for

Mercurians are Sales, Journalist, Public Speaker, Healer, and Therapist.

MANIFESTING YOUR POTENTIAL

Do you have great ideas that never see the light of day? Do you know seemingly ordinary people who seem to skate through life with things just falling into their lap? Your fingers tell the tale of where your potential lies. Your thumbs give clues as to the likelihood that your potential will be realized.

The size, shape, flexibility and strength of your thumbs indicate your innate capacity for getting results. A careful study of your thumbs, relative to your hand, indicates your level of determination, sphere of influence and capacity for manifesting your potential.

RIGHT VS LEFT

Does it make a difference which hand is being read? Ideally, both will be read. The right hand indicates how you show up in the outer world. The side of your personality that's displayed to your outer circle of associates will show up in your right hand. Left hand markings tell the story of how you relate to close friends and family, your inner circle. Rarely do both hands show the same markings.

ELEMENTAL HAND SHAPES

You can learn a lot about yourself and others by simply paying attention to the shape of the hands. The picture below shows the 4 main elemental hand shape types. Most people will be a blend of types rather than a textbook example of a single type.

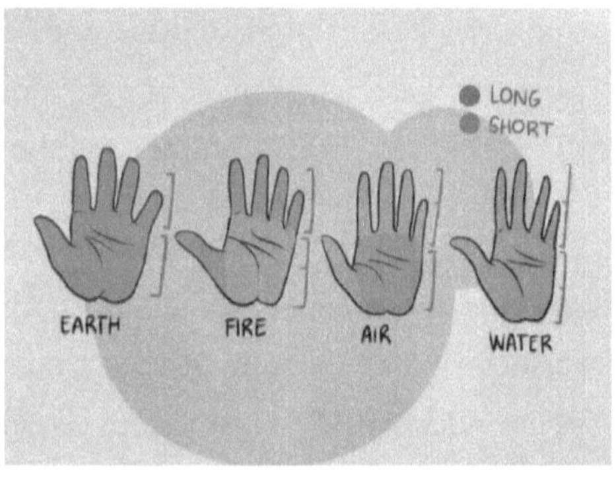

To determine your elemental hand shape type, look at your hand and compare it to the picture above. The length of your fingers relative to the length of your palm determines which hand shape type best represents you.

For example, if your palm is short and somewhat square and your fingers are shorter than your palm, your elemental hand shape is considered to be Earth. Earth element, like the earth beneath your feet, is stable and slow to change. Personality traits of the Earth element are down-to-earth, likes consistency,

feels connected to nature, plants and animals, loyal
and somewhat resistant to change.

MAJOR LINES

Take a look at your palm. Do you see lots of fine
lines going in every which direction, very few lines
deeply etched into the hand or something in between?

These lines represent different energies that you carry.
Unlike your fingerprints which never change, the lines
in your hands can change size, shape, and/or direction
or even disappear and reappear over time. The lines
in your hands literally reflect your thought processes
and brain activity over time. Lines that are strong and
clear will offer the best flow of energy.

Since this is an overview chapter on hand reading,
only 3 major lines – Heart, Head and Life will be
discussed.

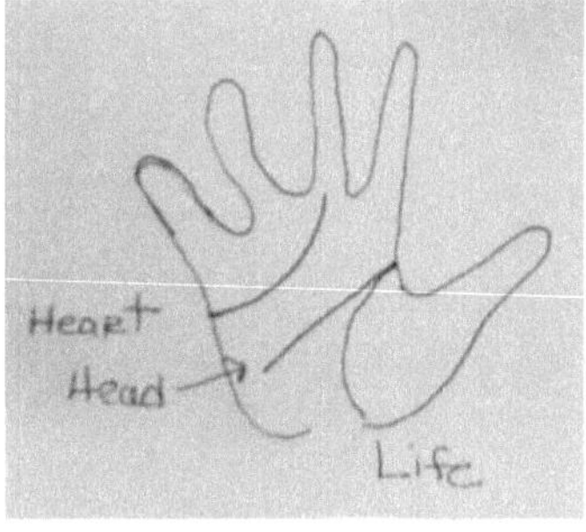

HEART LINE

Looking for love in all the wrong places? Do the same issues come up in your relationships over and over again? Understanding your relationship needs as well as how others are likely to treat you can go a long ways towards achieving relationship harmony.

The Heart Line is the one that starts on the outer edge of the palm, under the pinkie finger, and runs horizontally across the palm. It usually ends somewhere in the area under the pointer or middle finger. The Heart Line tells us what emotional filters we run our life experiences through.

The longer your Heart Line, the more time you are likely to spend in the world of emotions. Longer Heart Lines typically belong to those who put others needs before their own – sometimes to their own detriment. The curvier your Heart Line, the more likely you are to express your feelings to the outside world.

There are 4 main Heart Line types which are pictured below. How do your Heart Lines compare?

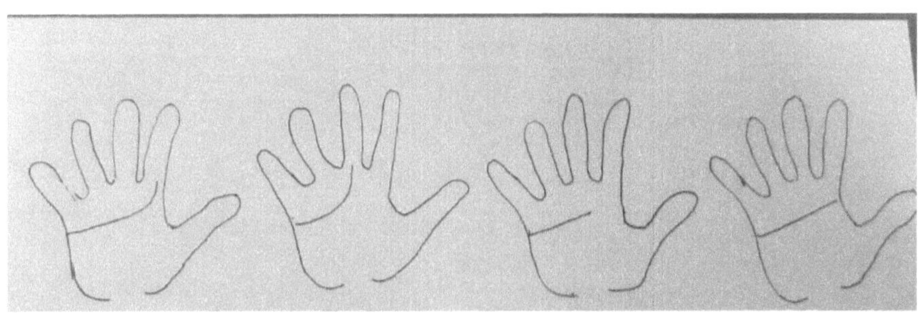

HEAD LINE

The Head Line is the horizontal line that usually runs across the middle of the hand. It starts from the inside edge of the palm below the Jupiter finger and above the thumb. The Head Line travels toward the outer edge of the palm.

The Head Line reflects your mental processing. The longer the line, the more time you're likely to spend thinking and mentally processing. The shorter the Head Line, the quicker the thinking. The cleaner and clearer the line, the cleaner and clearer the thinking. A messy Head Line will indicate scattered thinking. A straight Head Line indicates a tendency towards more

113

logical thinking. A curvy Head Line is indicative of more creative and/or emotional thinking.

How would you describe the thought processes of the owner of the hand below.

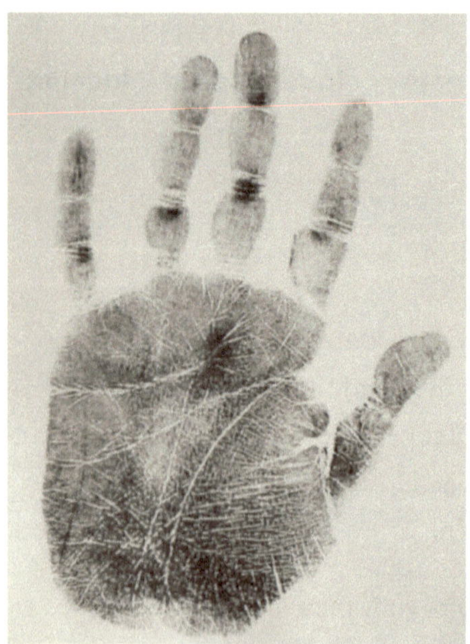

LIFE LINE

Like the Head Line, the Life Line starts on the inside edge of the palm below the Jupiter finger and above the thumb. The Life Line reflects family roots of origin, grounding to the earth and vitality. Repeat after me, **the Life Line does not indicate how long the owner will live.**

If you have a long Life Line, it indicates that you have vitality, strength and stamina. A short Life Line, on the other hand, represents feeling scattered. Short Life Lines are usually found on those who are still seeking to find their place in the world and lack a sense of connection. A healthy Life Line has a curve and a flow to it. A Life Line that appears flattened indicates a lack of ease in the owner's life.

How well-grounded do you think the owner of the hand below feels?

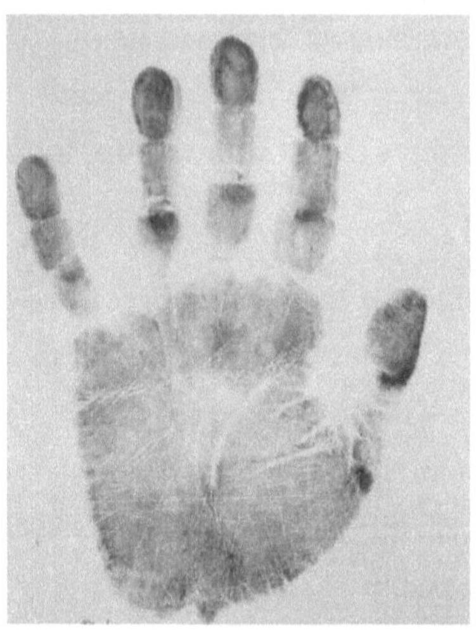

PUTTING IT ALL TOGETHER

The information presented in this chapter is only the tiniest tip of the iceberg with respect to what you can learn about yourself by having your hands read. With hand reading, it's absolutely essential to consider the information in **all** of the markings and how they interact versus picking a single feature and trying to draw conclusions. Using the hand below as an example…

We see someone who is practical, down-to-earth and loyal to their friends and family. They're a bit on the stubborn side perhaps and not likely to be an early adopter of trendy ideas. One of their strengths will be their communication skills which will be direct and straightforward. No overly flowery prose or lengthy explanations from this individual. They have a reasonably good ability to manifest their potential but need to be careful to lay the groundwork before taking action. At the time this print was taken they were not terribly interested in putting themselves out into the world. Structure and routine were also high priorities. This appears to be a very practical individual, not given to emotional display. Engaging in manual work or working outside would suit this person. In relationships, they spend most of their time talking about the weather or their day, not their feelings.

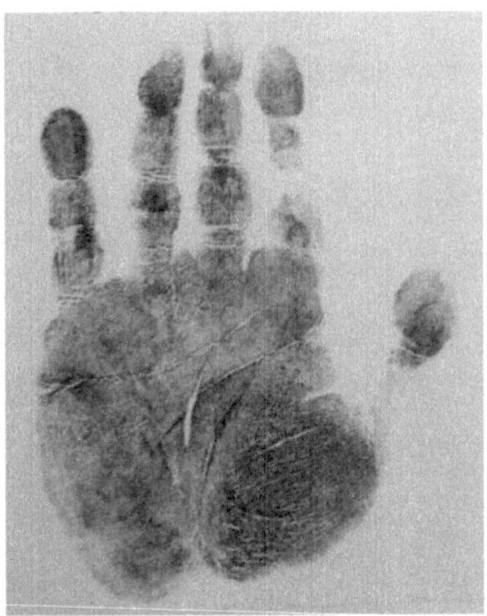

Fingerprints: L – Whorl, Composite Whorl, Peacock, Whorl, Loop

R – Whorl, Whorl, Loop, Whorl, Loop

Overall this person has the potential to be a successful leader. A big challenge for them will be to take risk and think outside the box. They are on the Life Path of Service. Acquiring and sharing knowledge of a practical nature will be their "happy place." Their Life Challenge will be addressing their feelings of "Am I worthy of Love?" Will they bury themselves with work or chasing success to avoid dealing with their feelings?

With hand reading, as with any self-awareness discipline, the person doing the reading will be interpreting the information through the filters of their own life experience. Choose wisely.

Marcella Theeman is a Certified Level 3 Hand Analyst through the American Academy of Hand Analysis. If you would like clarity about the way forward in life and love, Marcella can be reached for a reading at mptwindsock@hotmail.com or 541-816-0674.

History of Tarot
And other cards

Tarot cards have their start farther back than the 14th century. They were first used not as a spiritual or divining tool but as a game known as 'tarocchi appropriate'.

Players would be dealt cards and then use the theme associated with the cards to write poetic verses about the other players.

The cards spread throughout Europe where they became another game. It was much like our modern day bridge card game. Today a modern deck of Tarot cards has 79 cards. It consists of two groups of cards that are used in different ways to look into the future. One group is 'major arcana' and has 22 cards in that group. The other group is 'minor arcana' and has 56 cards in it.

In Italy wealthy families would pay an artist to hand paint decks of cards for them. These cards usually had suits of cups, swords, coins and polo sticks on them. Later Kings, Queens and other cards were introduced into the deck.

The cards and their meanings started to change in the 16th and early 17th centuries. People were starting to assign specific names and meanings to the cards. This lead to people offering suggestions of how each card could tell people something about themselves or the future.

By the 18th century "reading Tarot cards" was becoming a popular way to get answers to questions very quickly.

It was in 1782 that a French Freemason and former Protestant minister published a complexed analysis of the Tarot. This is when he revealed that the symbolism in the Tarot was in fact derived from the esoteric secrets of Egyptian Priests.

This man's name was Antoine Court de Gebelin. He went on to explain that an ancient occult had revealed the knowledge to Rome, the Catholic Church and the popes years earlier. The church had hidden this information and wanted to keep this arcane knowledge a secret. However when Antoine's book was published it revealed everything and went on to explain how to use the cards.

The meaning of the divination of the cards has changed over time. These changes are shaped by each era's culture and the needs of individual users.

In the 1700's it was believed that the Tarot cards originated from the legendary Book of Thoth. Thoth was an Egyptian god and the book was thought to be his property. Thoth was considered the god of wisdom. Tarot card readers found that by linking the Tarot to Egyptian mysticism, it gave the cards greater credibility. No one knows for sure if the Tarot was used in Egypt as a mystical tool or a card game.

Today you can get Tarot cards in almost any design you want.

Many people liked cards with birds and other animals on them. Their meanings where eventually taken from the deep beliefs Native Americans had in animals, animal totems, the Great Spirit and Mother Earth.

The word "medicine" in the Native American way means "anything that improves one's connection to the body, mind or spirit". People started to understand that nature and animals had powers they didn't. Because each animal in the Native way has its own power and magic, people wanted to call on that power for themselves.

When you use Medicine cards, you are calling upon the power of nature and specifically an animal or species. They bring with them their own wisdom and understanding about the Universe, or Great Mystery and how it works.

Even before the White Man started using medicine cards the Native Americans had a connection to the "medicine" and didn't need the cards to get their messages. All they needed to do was to walk with nature and they received their answers from the real animals. The White Man is the one that needs the cards to see the messages the animals bring to us.

Tarot and Oracle cards have been used for thousands of years in some way. However when you are using Medicine cards (specifically the Navajo cards) you are channeling animal totem power and teachings about your life's path.

Medicine cards, Tarot cards and Oracles cards can all be an advanced tool for personal growth, not just answering questions. They can show you how all of us are connected to each other, animals and Mother Earth.

The following chapter is written by a friend and client and how she uses Medicine cards. I think you will find her story very interesting. Also her bio is in the back of the book along with mine so you can find out more about her and her life.

Animal Medicine Cards

Connection to Universal Energy History

By Wendie Kause

For millions of years, we humans have used divination tools to connect to the unknown, unseen aspects of our relative human experience. The use of these tools, such as Tarot Cards, Pendulums, Runes, Crystals, and many more, is the attempt to understand and gain a deeper meaning of our physical existence.

Today we still use these sacred tools. They may look a bit different than they did thousands or even millions of years ago, but they are used for precisely the same reason. To help connect us to the Universal Energy and the Natural World.

In these modern times, it is more difficult to have access to Sacred Spaces or Sacred Elders to help teach us. As humans, we are so unwaveringly creative, we have developed many alternatives to achieve the innate desire to connect. Fundamentally we all understand that there is "More" to this physical world than we know. I like to call it "The Mystery."

How it Works

While we may not be able to scientifically prove our energetic connection to The Mystery, we can understand its physics. Without going into a boring physics or quantum physics lesson, let me explain in a nutshell how I understand the energetic connection to All things.

"Energy has no beginning, no end. It can never be destroyed. it is only ever shifting states." Panache Desai. I love the simple way this is described by Desai.

All things are made of Energy. This includes sound, light, and all material. The frequency and vibration of that Energy form the density of the material. An example, a stone vibrates at a much lower and different vibrational frequency than a cloud. Still, it's primarily created by the same Energy. Like humans and stars, we are the same, only vibrating on a different frequency.

If Energy is everything, and Energy has no beginning and no end and can never be destroyed, everything has to be connected. This includes time and space.

Therefore, any use of divination tools, allows us to tap into the universal Energy that surrounds us and is part of us.

I do not believe the "Power" is in the "Tools" we use, only that it is connected to us, and when we focus our Energy, it then becomes like a pencil. The pencil is not the writer, it is a tool to allow us to communicate our thoughts to others. The Medicine Cards are like the pencil, it " enables a conduit between our thoughts and our relative world experience.

How I Use Animal Medicine Cards

The tools I use the most are Animal Medicine cards and muscle testing. In this chapter, I am going to discuss the cards. I will tell you more about muscle testing in my next chapter. I have used the cards for over 20 years. They have helped me to connect with the natural animal energy that surrounds all of us.

My deck, Medicine Cards, The Discovery of Power through the Ways of Animals, written by Jamie Sams & David Carson in 1988, is my favorite. I recently purchased a new deck Animal Spirit, The Wild Unknown, written by Kim Krans. I enjoy them, but have only had them for a short while and do not feel as comfortable with them. I am enjoying the process of becoming familiar and confident using them, however.

I feel the energetic connection whenever I handle them. For me, animals, nature, and water seem to be the tools that connect me most to The Mystery. I say this to let you know, whatever divination tool you prefer is right. You'll know what is right for you by how easily you can connect and resonate with the readings. There is no right or wrong deck or tool to use to connect you to the Universal Energy.

There are several ways to use the cards. There are standard layouts that serve to answer questions that you may have or enlighten you on the whys of things. Each set comes with detailed descriptions for layout and general use of the cards.

A popular layout is inquiring about the Past, Present, and Future. By gaining a new or different perspective on Past, Present, and Future, you may be able to look at a circumstance with a different attitude. You may have always thought it was a negative encounter. Once you have considered it from a different point of view, you may come to the realization that the situation is actually an incredible gift of learning. You may find yourself filled with gratitude for the experience. Furthermore, this new perspective may allow you to make better decisions for your future.

Another character of the cards helps you to find your Animal Spirits or Totems. This is the animal guide or helper that supports you in this incarnation. There are different Totems for different aspects of your life; Primary Guide, Spiritual, Creative, Counsel, Dreamtime, Heart, and Happiness, Overcoming Challenges, Male and Female Energy, and Balance. These are the animals that represent the Energy you can draw from to assist you in these areas of your life. Some you choose mindfully and others you pull from the deck randomly. My Primary Animal Spirit is Turtle. It was given to me via Universal Energy. In other words, I randomly drew that card after I sat quietly for a bit and asked for guidance. Turtle is "Mother Earth." In Native American teachings, it is the oldest symbol for planet Earth. It is the personification of goddess energy and the eternal Mother, from which our lives evolve. We are born of the womb of Earth, and to her soil, our bodies will return. In honoring the Earth, we are asked by Turtle to be mindful of the cycle of give and take, to give back to the Mother as she has given us." This is an excerpt from the book, Medicine Cards, Page 77.

Whenever I feel lost or unsure of my direction, I turn to my Turtle Totem Energy to guide me.

Meditation and Focus

Another powerful way to use these cards is to sit quietly, take a few deep breaths to settle your mind and body. With no specific question in mind, I ask The Mystery to provide me with a powerful message. As I make the request, I gently handle the cards and shuffle them. When ready, I pick a card at random. I then use the animal spirit energy of the card drawn to focus my meditation. If it's dear, I know I need to be gentle and brave. If it is the wolf, I realize I need to help teach, lead, or make a definite final decision on something I may be considering.

Plans and Goals

Towards the end of the year, I begin to plan and set goals for the next. I sit down and focus on the upcoming year, I then ask, "What animal energy will best assist me through the year?" In November 2019, I pulled Buffalo. Considering the outcome so far in 2020, I am grateful for Buffalo Energy to help guide me through these turbulent times of COVID-19 and global unrest. "The Buffalo sees challenge, hardship, or a bump in the road as an opportunity for upliftment.

Therefore the Buffalo does not fear, death, illness, or misfortune...its gentle eyes look to the road ahead, trusting every turn." Excerpt from Animal Spirit, The Wild Unknown, Page 75. With extreme gratitude, I embrace this Energy whenever I begin to feel fearful, full of anxiety, and worry about the future.

While planning for the next year, I contemplate my annual social media calendar. I pull a card for each month. I grab my calendar and write the Animal Spirit that I pulled at the top of each month. I use it as a boost to create content for the month. For example, if I pull Rabbit for January, the content I create will represent overcoming anxiety and fear. Rabbit Medicine is Fear. If Beaver Medicine is pulled for February, I know I will focus my content on creativity, building, and projects to get started or finish. Beaver medicine is the "Builder." I do this for each month, and it helps me to focus and make decisions on what I wish to create that month. Note: I do not always follow the represented content I pulled during my planning process. Be aware that things change, new ideas manifest! I do not believe we should allow anything to stand in the way of our creativity that manifests itself in the here and now.

Using the cards for Readings

This, to me, can become a slippery slope of egotism. There are times I use the cards, with the permission of my clients, to guide them. I am careful to realize that, just like with my coaching, I am the guide, not the doer of the activities adopted by my clients. It is not I who helped them to manifest success. They are the creators of their life experiences. Not I. I consider myself a tool or map if you prefer, that they can use to guide them along their own path.

At some point, you may decide to utilize the cards to assist others. Please keep in mind that it is not You who delivers the messages or the motivation for the other. It is the Universal Energy that flows through you. Suppose you begin to believe You are the power? In that case, you also need to take responsibility, if the person you are helping decides not to walk the path they are guided to. None of us has the power to make another do, be, and have something we deem appropriate. It is up to the individual to pick and choose their path.

We are each part of the tapestry of life. Set aside your expectations for a specific outcome when providing readings to others. You are the guide, not a conjurer making the other do what the cards reveal. If you follow this simple guideline, you will not get lost in the egoic and sometimes disastrous outcome of becoming a profit for profit.

In whatever way you choose to utilize this magnificent tool, allow gratitude, honor, and respect.

Witchcraft

It is unclear as to when witches and witchcraft started to be recognized. The earliest records of witches are in the Bible in1 Samuel that was thought to be written between 931 BC and 721 BC.

The writing is a story of King Saul who sought out the Witch of Endor to summon the dead prophet Samuel to help him defeat the Philistine army. The witch brought forward the spirit of Samuel but it wasn't what Saul thought it would be.

Samuel prophesied that Saul and his sons would not be successful and all would die. According to the Bible, the next day Saul's sons died in battle and Saul then committed suicide.

There are other stories about witches in the Bible but the fact is, the Bible is not a very favorable place to read about witches. However, back then any spiritual tools, that weren't approved by the church, were thought as evil and part of the devil.

The book 'Malleus Malificarum' was published in 1486 by two German Dominicans. This book spurred witch mania for many years. The title translation is "The Hammer of Witches". It was a detailed guide on how to identify, hunt and interrogate witches. The

'Malleus Malificarum' became the authority for Protestants and Catholics to flush out witches. The book was a best seller for more than 100 years.

The first witch that was put to death was long before the witch trials in America in 1692. Witch hysteria took over in Europe in the mid 1400's. Alse Young was the first witch to be put to death in this time period in England. This was really the start of witch mania and lasted almost two hundred years in Europe.

As witch mania started to die out in England it was just starting to heat up in the new America. 1626 thru 1730 almost everyone in the new America was looking for a witch to blame for everything that was going wrong.

Many accused witches confessed after being tortured. The next hundred years was really a "witch hunt" time in history. Many innocent people were burnt at the stake or hung. Hundreds were accused and many thrown into jail.

Bridget Bishop was the first person executed in America at the Salem witch trials in 1692. In those trials there were 14 women, 5 men and one six year old girl put to death. Single women, widows and women who were on the outer margins of society were targeted.

What is ironic is the word "witch" comes from the Saxon word "Wicca" that means "wise one." There is nothing in the meaning of the word "witch" to even suggest there is anything evil about it.

At this time, the tension from the wars between the French and British, the attacks from Native Americans and the small pox epidemic made everyone in America looking for a scapegoat. The people were in a panic situation and the timing was perfect for everyone to look for a witch who was probably the cause of all if this disorder.

The witch trials of 1692 were spurred by young girls that had body contortions, fits and uncontrolled screaming. (Today it's believed that the girls had a reaction to being poisoned by a fungus.) These actions caused people to panic even more. They started looking for any reason to accuse others of being witches whether they interacted with the girls are not.

There was another famous witch, Grace Sherwood and what they did to her helped turn the tide on the witch mania. She was accused of killing pigs and putting a hex on cotton fields.

The way the court decided to test her to determine her guilt or innocence was the big turning point in how to tell if someone was a witch.. Her arms and legs were bound and she was thrown into a lake. If she sunk, she was innocent; if she floated she was guilty. She floated and was thrown into jail for the next eight years.

An article was published about how ridiculous some witchcraft accusations were and how so many had been wrongly convicted. This article made people think and the mania died down. There were even laws passed to help protect people from being wrongly targeted and accused of witchcraft.

Today many witches are still living under the historical stereotype of being evil. Most witches today practice Wicca, which is recognized as an official religion in the US and Canada.

Wiccans avoid evil. Their motto is "harm none." They really try to live a peaceful, tolerant and balanced life; being one with nature, animals and humanity. They still perform witchcraft but there is seldom anything evil or dark about it.

They usually use the Book of Shadows, which is a collection of wisdom and witchcraft. It is equal to a prayer book that other religions might have. Most potions now are more herb mixtures to help with colds, flu or allergies. Even in the past it's believed that most people accused of witchcraft were using it for healing and protection against evil.

Just like everything else on this planet, there is or can be a dark side to witchcraft. Some people believe that if they use it for hexes and curses it will give them power. The only thing they are doing is creating extremely bad karma for themselves.   There is also a saying for anyone who is wondering about curses; 'if you don't believe in them, they have no power over you'. You are the one that has to take that energy in and be afraid of it for it to work. So these people are just hurting their own lives more than they are anyone else.

There are still some countries in these modern times that believe witches are evil and will beat them to death. (It is thought that the green faces of witches at Halloween came about because people beat them in the head and the green and black represents the bruises on their faces.)

Even though Wicca is not really associated with fortune telling, it is a very spiritual path. Many of their spells and potions have to do with working with energy to make a better future. Many Wiccans are very intuitive and/or psychic.

Not all witches are Wiccans and not all Wiccans are witches.

Also, Wiccans are pagans but not all Pagans are Wiccan – are you confused yet. It's like Baptist is a

subset of being Christian. Wicca is a religion –
witchcraft is a practice.

Witchcraft has several different beliefs or methods of
doing applications or spells. Some witches think the
power is in the candles, oils, flowers, salt and other
elements and tools they use. Some witches believe the
power is in the intent that is in their heart when they
are doing a spell.

Remember the Wicca religion is a healing religion
and to harm none. Anyone can join the Wicca
religion but to become a real witch takes a lot of work
and studying. You will probably need a mentor also.
A person who is already a witch can teach you what to
do and how to do it so you don't get yourself into
trouble with negative energy.

Witchcraft can help you make wiser choices and
bring in positive energy to help you work toward a
better future.

Other ways to tell your future and fortune

In this chapter we are going to look at some of the oldest forms of looking into the future or getting messages from the other side.

Spodomancy is a form of divination by reading ashes, soot or cinders. These left over elements are usually from a ritual or sacrificial fire. The patterns that form in ashes of burnt offerings from a sacrificial fire is called "tephromancy".

Tephromancy is the practice of reading ashes from burnt offerings, usually an animal, and spodomancy is the practice of reading ashes from other burnt elements.

The word spodomancy is from the Greek words 'spodos' means "wood ash" and 'mentcia' means "prophecy".

Here too, there were several ways to read the askes depending on what country or area you lived in.

In the Middle Ages the method went something like the following.

If the cinders were hollow and oblong they were known as 'coffins' indicating death; oval cinders were called 'cradles' indicating something around a child; round cinders were called 'purses' and indicated prosperity and heart-shaped were of course a sign of a lover.

However if you were in Scotland and a piece of soot fell out of the chimney at a wedding breakfast it was bad luck for the couple.

Still another method was to spread the ashes out from a ritual fire and leave them overnight. The reading of the ashes would be in the morning by reading what letters that might have formed and are readable and which ones had faded away.

Another method would be to read the ashes of a sacrificial fire after the fire is out. The diviner looks for the letters and/or symbols that might have formed.

This practice of fortune telling is extremely ancient and may well have had its beginnings with prehistoric man. This is because of their fascination of fire and not understanding how it really worked.

Pyromancy is the divination by flames or fire. The basic form is where the diviner observes flames from a ritual fire, candle or other flame source. The diviner interprets any shapes they see in the flames.

The following are several variations on how the fire can be used.

Alomancy is throwing salt into the flames to get different shapes and colors. Then these will be read for the diviner.

Botanomancy is burning plants compared to a sacrifice or wood.

Capnomancy is reading the smoke more than the flames.

Causimancy is burning several things at once, like plants, paper, wood, etc. and reading the flames.

Daphnomancy is burning only Laurel tree leaves.

Osteonancy is burning bones to produce cracking in the bones which will be read for the future or the past. Thought to have started in Africa.

Plastromancy is using turtle plastrons which is the bottom part of a turtle's shell.

Scaputimancy is burning the scapulae to read it.

Sideromancy is burning a straw with an iron and reading the flame.

Pyromancy is considered one of the earliest forms of reading by fire to tell the future and fortunes. It started as animals were sacrificed to the gods. It was thought that through these fires and the flames and finally the ashes that the gods were giving messages to humans. Thank God the Pythagoreans came up with a vegetable form because they disapproved of shedding any blood which saved many lives.

Many times if there seems to be nothing happening in the flames, other elements might be thrown into the fire to make the flames jump and turn colors. An example might be throwing pitch or a powder of some kind into the fire. All changes in the fire as far as colored flames, crackling sparks and anything else were all considered a part of the message from the gods.

Libanomancy is primarily reading incense smoke and could include the way the incense ash falls. This way of fortune telling is ancient and there are manuals to learn how to do it that come from Babylonian around 2000-1600 BC.

This was a very popular way to receive messages from all the gods or spirits on the other side. It traveled from Mesopotamia to Egypt and later into Europe. As new ways emerged to tell fortunes, the reading of fire, flames and ashes started to die out. However the Babylonians recorded the many different meanings and interpretations of the fires, flames, ashes and even the smoke.

So getting to know what smoke or flames can tell you is a very real and ancient way of telling your future or talking to the gods. It also means you have to study the writings of the ancient Babylonian people.

More Ways to Get Messages
About your Life

<u>Face readings</u> is an art that the Chinese specialize in. This form of divination breaks up the face into thirteen different sections. They also study the brow line, the eyes, eyebrows, nose, chin and other aspects of the face. All of this can help them tell you about you and your future.

<u>Parrot Astrology</u> is used in India and Singapore. Green parrots are trained to pick out a Tarot card after the diviner lays them out on the ground. The card the parrot picks will have your answer.

<u>Obi divination</u> is a type of fortune telling that is popular with African psychics. They throw stones, shells or nuts and then read the information they get from the pattern. This is a very old practice that originated within the Yoruba tradition which is part of Nigeria.

<u>Throwing bones</u> is a practice linked to Africa, Asia and North America. Chicken bones are the most popular bones to use. A circle is drawn on the ground and the cooked, clean bones are thrown into the circle. Then the diviner makes the reading from how the bones landed on the ground.

Abocomancy is a practice of reading dust, sand or salt. The diviner will read the shapes in these elements to tell the future.

Geomancy can be used with abocomancy. Geomancy is the study of Earth and animals. An example would be seeing a rabbit walk or run in front of you. A grid would be divided over the area where the rabbit ran and would be interpreted by a diviner that is trained in geomancy.

Apantomancy is using things or animals you come across by chance to receive a message or answer to something you asked earlier in the day or week. You can interpret these things as signs from the Universe, God or Goddess, etc. These signs usually mean something personal to the person that sees them. It would be like seeing a black cat. Some people would say that it's a "no" to their question. Others might think it means good luck and a positive answer. Still others might see it as a message from a loved one that has crossed.

Arithmancy and numerology work together. Most of us know that numerology is the study of numbers and interpreting them in conjunction with our lives. Numerology is assigning a spiritual significance to

certain numbers. Arithmancy is the act of analyzing
the numbers to get an answer.

The Greeks would assign values to the letters in the
names of their enemies to foretell the outcome of a
battle.

  Augury is the practice of telling the future based on
the movement of birds. There are several different
ways to do this. One is divining birds in flight.
Another is watching them on the ground. Yet another
is to throw them some food and see how they eat it.

  Belomancy is telling your future by using arrows.
This was even mentioned in the Bible so we know it is
an ancient practice. One way of doing this is to have
different colored arrows and put them in a quiver on
your back so you can't see them or the colors. Ask
your question and then randomly pull one arrow out
of the quiver. Of course you will have to assign an
answer to each color first. Like white is yes and black
is no. The other way to do this is to shoot a couple of
arrows into the air and watch how they might cross
each other's path or how they land on the ground.

  Bibleomancy is using books to get your messages.
This is usually using spiritual or religious books or
even the Bible. It's easy to practice and the more you
do it, the more messages you will start receiving. All
you need to do is ask a question and then open the

book. Read a sentence or paragraph that you opened
up too. There should be an answer in what you are
reading.

   Casting is somewhat like Osteomancy, the throwing
of bones. Casting involves charms and casting them
out onto a divination board.

   Ceromancy is using melted wax. You need to ask
your question before you light the candle. After it is
lit, wait until the wax is melting and some has pooled.
Pour the hot wax into a bowl of cold water to cool it.
When it has hardened, take the entire amount of wax
out and read the shape in relation to your question.

   Chirognomy is the practice of reading a person's
hand based on the shape, length of the fingers and the
back of the hand as well as the side and palm. This is
not a palm reading as this more detailed and using
more than just the palm.

   Cledonism is taking what you hear as a message. It
is in the same class with apantomancy as it can be
viewed as seeing/hearing signs from the gods and
loved ones. Here is an example of what might happen
to get a message. You ask a question to the Universe
and no one else. Then later in the day a person walks
up to you and seems to tell you something that
answers your question. Another example is in
Homer's Odyssey, Odyssey hears thunder right after

asking for a sign from the gods and he takes the thunder as approval from Zeus.

Conchomancy is placing a seashell to your ear and analyzing the sounds you hear from it.

Dactylomancy is a Greek word meaning 'finger divination'. You put a ring on a string and then ask your question. Lift the ring up until it's suspended in the air. You can then interpret a 'yes' or 'no' or 'maybe' by the way it swings or sways.

Dice can be used to fortune tell. Two or three dice are needed. After you have asked your question, roll the dice. If all the dice land on odd numbers the answer is 'no'. Even numbers on all the dice mean 'yes'. A mix of odd and even means 'uncertain' at this time.

Dobutsu Uranai is a modern fortune telling practice in Japan. It is a form of using a horoscope or astrology. There are 12 signs and you are assigned your sign by using your birth date. The 12 signs are animals: lion, sheep, koala, panther, wolf, cheetah, monkey, tiger, Pegasus, elephant, raccoon and fawn. Each animal has its own meaning and that meaning will be able to tell you about your future.

Dominos have been used for years around the world and is somewhat like dice. You ask your question and pull two tiles from a pile of them. Then the numbers

on the two tiles are interpreted. Two blank tiles
predict bad luck however two sixes mean happiness
and success. Everything in between is interpreted by
the size of the number and if they match or not.

Faromancy is reading the way beans or peas fall. Its
origin is believed to be in the Middle East. Today it is
still used in Bosnia and some places in Russia.

Graphology is studying handwriting. Even though
it has become a science, it can still be used to divine a
person's future. This would take some studying to
make sure you understand the many different styles of
handwriting and what they mean.

Haruspicy involves using entrails, mainly liver, of
sacrificial animals. It is an ancient practice that was
started in Mesopotamia and was used from 900-600
BC. There are very specific instruction on how it is
done and what it means. Luckily this practice has not
been practiced for a very long time.

Iching is probably the best known Chinese fortune
telling method in the US. It involves throwing coins
several times, noticing how they land and then
interpreting the pattern they created based on the
Book of Changes.

Jiaobei/Poe is popular in Taiwan and used in their
Taoist temples. Two 'moon blocks' are thrown on the

ground. The position they land in will give you your answer. This is typically a 'yes' or 'no'.

<u>Lithomancy</u> is the use of stones such as crystal, amethyst, tiger's eye and rose quartz. Each stone has a meaning to help you work through events in your life. An example would be if you picked a rose quartz it would tell you there are heart issues and/or love. You will need ten or more different stones. Each stone has a different meaning. You put them in a bag, ask your question and pull one stone out. That stone and what it symbolizes will give you a possible outcome.

<u>Mi Kayu Ura</u> is a Japanese practice that uses rice or beans and how they lay out. This is usually done fifteen days after the new moon.

<u>Mirror scrying</u> is associated with the Mesoamerican culture. It is similar to crystal ball scrying, which is staring into the mirror or ball.

<u>Molcosophy</u> interprets good or bad luck through the shape of a mole and where it is on the body.

<u>Necromancy</u> is using spirits of people or animals who have crossed over. There is usually some kind of ritual involved so it is classified as a type of magic or witchcraft.

<u>Nggam</u> is a Cameroonian method using the movements of crabs and/or spiders. The only way to learn the right way to do this is to go to Cameroon. The Mambila people will teach you because if you make up your own interpretations, you will be wrong.

O-Mikuji involves randomly selecting a scroll of paper that has a pre-written prophecy on it. These scrolls are available to visitors at Japanese shrines and temples. They will offer you one after you give them a donation. The prophecy is supposed to be just for you.

Ogham is using rods engraved with a letter from the Ogham alphabet. The alphabet is an ancient language so each letter has its own meaning and that meaning will give you an answer.

Phrenology is no longer used. It was a method where measurements of the skull could tell someone's health, character and temperament. Those traits could then be interpreted to tell their future.

Rhabdomancy uses rods or stick. Belomancy and dowsing rods are a subdivision of Rhabdomancy.

Teraphim was a practice using small idols. However, their function and meaning have been lost throughout time.

In the end
Or maybe just the beginning

I have tried to include most of the ways humans have tried or practiced to see into the future or find their fortune. Some are a lost art. Some just didn't work and were abandoned for new practices. Still others are alive and well and are with us today. Some are easy to do and some have great rituals and need time and teachers.

There are hundreds of ways humans have used to try and see into the future throughout time. The one thing that most of them have in common is the belief; energy and intent put into them seem to help the outcome. People who use these tools have to have to believe that in some way they help bring in messages from loved ones or the Universe to help guide us on our path.

Most people that use these tools have some kind of gift to help them "read or hear" the messages that are brought forward. Intuitiveness, clairvoyance, being psychic are gifts that all of us have in varying degrees. Some of us are meant to use them to help others and some of us are to use them for personal guidance. No matter what you do with your gift or the tools you use, make sure it's positive and remember that nothing is set in stone. Fortune telling is only a guideline.

In the end, it really doesn't matter what practice or method you use to help you see the future or help you on your path. What matters is what feels right to you. One method might work for you and doesn't work for your best friend and that's okay.

Follow that little voice in your head and that feeling in your gut. That is your intuition. Remember it's not your mother's, father's, friend's or anyone else's life, it's yours. Getting help to see into the future is natural and can help all of us see that there is a future and how good it can be.

You can do some of it yourself and then you can call someone like me to either validate the messages you received or to ask more questions to get more information. And remember, it's not how much someone charges that proves how good they are. Someone who charges less can be better than someone who charges more.

There will always be people who will abuse these tools or say they are a psychic and they aren't because they just want your money. Ask a person questions before you ask for a reading. If they seem upset or don't want to answer them, run! All good psychics will tell you how they work, what tools they might use and other questions about them.

There are some people that feel psychics should share their gift for free but that would put the energy exchange between the psychic and the client out of balance. The Universe is a balance of give and take and when there isn't an exchange of some kind, it will throw that energy out of balance. This can create karma or other problems.

Having a gift of any kind is how all of us make a living. You might be good at dancing and you teach dance. You might be good at singing and you make money by singing. All these gifts are looked at as a way to make a living and psychic readings are no different.

However, if you aren't good at them, people will see it and you will not make money. So if you decide to use any of the tools in this book, be good at them. Study, learn, and practice. Be the best you can be and always use it in a positive, loving way to be of service to all that may come to you.

Don't hurry through the instructions and think you know it all. None of us knows it all and if you hurry to fast, you will miss a step and then you will need to start over again. There is a responsibility to using any of these tools and you should take that responsibility very seriously. It is always an honor to allow a tool to help you connect with other energies. It's an honor that should never be taken for granted.

I leave you with this one last fact, not even psychics can always see their path or lessons. We are humans and sometimes we have to go through a lesson, just like everyone else, to learn and grow our soul. We might be able to see our path more clearly than most people but even the best psychic has a psychic friend they call on to help them once in a while.

I wish all of you good fortune and a positive and peaceful future.

Shirley Scott – Animal communicator/psychic

www.shirley-scott.com

sscott @shirley-scott.com

 Shirley is an internationally known animal communicator and clairvoyant. She does clairvoyant readings on both animals and people. She can also connect to love ones who have crossed. She received this gift after a near-death, out-of-body experience in 2000. This experience showed her that there is more to us than just our physical life. This experience led her to dive into the world of spirit and the world of unseen "mystery".

   She looks at life on a positive level, no matter what is happening. Life is full of lessons and she believes that every day we can learn a way to live a better life. She believes that our galaxy and the Universe will show us how to elevate our soul and our purpose while we are on Earth if we just open up to the messages we get.

She was the first dog trainer for the "Dogs in Prison" program at the Washington State Penitentiary in Walla Walla, Washington for four years. Her animal communication helped her pair dogs with inmates and to let the dogs know what was happening. She even taught a few of the inmates how to become animal communicators.

   She has written articles for Animal Wellness Magazine, Hedra News and other spiritual publications. Her books include;
'Religion vs. Spirituality – One Psychic's Point of View' points out the differences of religion and being spiritual;
'Conscious Dreaming – talking to the fairies' is a fantasy as Shirley is shrunk down to the size of a fairy and talks to them about life;
'Why she has to die' is her experience with domestic abuse;
'A Quick and Simple guide to ghosts & demons and how to deal with them' explain the differences between ghosts and demons and deal with a haunting or demon possession;

'Today I'm reminded' is a work book to help people think more positive;

'Talking to the dead, fortune and future telling' is a book about tools that have been used from the past to the present to talk to the dead or tell the future.

Her 3 CD's, **Face Your Fears - Change Your Life, Telepathy and Animal Communication,** and **Going Beyond Positive Thought** are teaching tools for everyone who wants to learn inner strength, positive thinking and how to live a better, more joyful life.

She runs a small animal rescue that helps find homes for unwanted and abused animals. Right now she has two goats, six cats and two dogs. The rescue helps find homes for animals before the animal has to go into a shelter by working with other organizations in the state. For more information or to donate please go to www.animalrescueranch.com   – it is a 501c3 so your donation is tax deductible.

She does workshops and speaking engagements on animal communication, telepathy and the world of seen and unseen energy. She teaches animal communication and how to become more intuitive. She can help you with pet issues, life issues, your health and help you get on and stay on a path that makes your life more spiritual, joyful and peaceful. She can point out karmic issues and help you understand why things are happening in your life.

Shirley does her readings over the phone from her home in Imnaha, Oregon where she lives in the woods.   Please visit her websites at www.shirley-scott.com to learn more and to set up an appointment with her.

Wendie Kause, (Pronounced "Cause")

Founder Kause Success Management

1806 Airway Ave.

Lewiston, ID 83501

208/305-6184 Website: www.kausesuccess.com
Email: wendie@kausesuccessmanagement.com
Podcast: https://wkause.podbean.com/

INTRODUCTION/BIO

Wendie Kause is the Founder of Kause Success. She inspires passion and transformation in individuals and entrepreneurs who gain knowledge, clarity, and confidence to manifest the life they desire.

She knows that everyone can have a happy and abundant lifestyle if only they would connect deeply with their higher self and align its purpose with inspired activity. She guides people step by step through the process of aligning their souls' purpose with external actions by offering direct tough love coaching, tailored strategies, and motivational speaking to uncover what's holding them back, slowing them down or stopping them from manifesting their full potential — then transforming those obstacles into bold, inspired action.

As a Business Coach for over seven years, she has helped and inspired hundreds of individuals and businesses get out of their own way and make positive changes that result in increased income, happier work culture, and improved customer service all resulting in increased profitability and team satisfaction.

The beginning of her entrepreneurial journey began partially because of a personal crisis; the loss of her mother to cancer followed a few years later by the death of her much loved step-daughter to illness. These losses propelled her forward to realize that life is too short to hold back because of fear or limiting beliefs.

While tragedy often thrusts us into action to make changes in our lives, she does not believe a crisis is the only way to make a shift. To create purposeful transformation in her life, she made a spiritual Pilgrimage, called El Camino De Santiago, or The Way, a 500-mile walk across Spain to see if she could inspire a shift in her life. And it did. She had a spiritual awakening that transformed her life. Her purpose now is to guide others to live a fully awakened life filled with curiosity, beauty, wonderment, and happiness.

FULL BIO

Wendie Kause is the Owner of Kause Success Management. She has lived in Lewiston, ID since 1991. She sought out and received employment in her area of expertise in the Relocation Industry getting hired within her first week in the Valley as Operations Manager at 3B's Moving and Storage, agent for Mayflower Transit. During her employ from 1991 to 2003, she received a certification from LCSC Workforce Training as an Outside Sales Professional. She also attended many training conferences focusing on sales and leadership as well as personal development.

In 2003 she began her new career as an Executive Sales Representative at IdaVend Broadcasting. In 2009 she was promoted to Local Sales Manager, and because of her excellence in leadership, During her time at Idavend, she received extensive sales and leadership training and earned her certification as a Radio Sales Manager.

In October of 2011, she left Idavend to start her own business and opened her coaching practice in January of 2012. In 2013 she earned a certification in Multi-Cultural Communications. She has also been published twice in an online publication – Pulse for Linked In.

Wendie has spent over 30 years purposefully developing her signature coaching approach that she offers to her clients today. When she discovered that she had a talent for leading, inspiring, and motivating people, she created and learned techniques that enabled her to share her strategic concepts and skills with individuals, companies, colleges, universities and economic development centers. Since she opened her practice her focus has been on sales, leadership and customer service. With her assistance her clients represent a bottom-line increase of over 20 million dollars in combined commissions and increased sales.

In 2017 she decided to take her business in a new direction, she now brings her time and talent to inspire Passionate Transformational Visionaries to gain knowledge, clarity, and confidence to start or grow their own business and manifest their true purpose. She does this by turning fear into curiosity, teaching the art of selling and manifesting their wildest dreams through personal development, and connecting with their higher self. She believes that our ultimate purpose reveals itself when we understand that we each are in charge of our destiny and are the creators of our lives.

Wendie understands the importance of giving back to the community that she loves. She was instrumental in the development of the now flourishing Beautiful Downtown Lewiston and served on the Board of Directors for Lewis Clark Valley Chamber of Commerce 2013-2015 and currently; Board Member of The Salvation Army, Hands of Hope Program. Wendie is heavily involved in supporting military veterans as an Auxiliary Member of the Combat Veterans Motorcycle Association (CVMA-13-3). She is heavily involved with the American Warfighters, a Veterans Non-Profit organization that was started by her husband and partners. As the wife of a National Guardsman (RT) who served in Iraq and a step-mom to two beautiful sons, she has a unique understanding and perspective of the needs of military veterans and their families.

Wendie is married to Joseph Kause and has two stepsons, Trever and Conner and is Mother to Jack Russel, Hailey and Pit Bull, Reilly.

208/305-6184

Lewiston, ID

www.kausesuccess.com